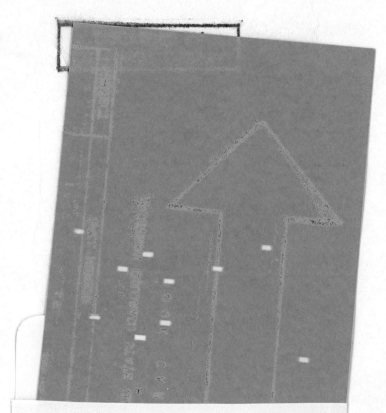

Southern Colorado State College
Pueblo, Colorado

DATE DUE		
FEB 29 '68		
MAR 2 6 '69		
MAY 5 '69		
MAY 1 9 '69		
JUN 3 '69		

NEIGHBORS
IN A
NEW WORLD

The Organization of American States

The Pan American Union, the "House of the Americas"

Neighbors
in a
New World:

THE ORGANIZATION OF
AMERICAN STATES

Ruth Karen

THE WORLD PUBLISHING COMPANY

CLEVELAND AND NEW YORK

Published by the World Publishing Company
2231 West 110th Street, Cleveland 2, Ohio
Published simultaneously in Canada by
Nelson, Foster & Scott Ltd.
Library of Congress catalog card number: 66-13905
HL

CONTENTS

"For we are made for cooperation,
like feet, like hands, like eyelids,
like the rows of the upper and lower teeth.
To act against one another then is contrary to nature:
And it is acting against another
To be vexed and to turn away."

The Meditations of MARCUS AURELIUS

NEIGHBORS
IN A
NEW WORLD

The Organization of American States

THE HOUSE
OF THE
AMERICAS

About midway between the White House and
the Washington Monument a driveway curves around a
jade-green lawn shadowed by cedars and double-blossom
cherry trees, silver sycamores and cones of blue spruce. The
asphalt arch sweeps to a building with tall balconied windows, wine-red tile roof, and a white marble face cut by
three vaulted doors of wrought bronze.

A narrow stone band above the gates bears the legend,
in chiseled gold letters: PAN AMERICAN UNION.

Pan American Union is a twofold concept. It defines an
idea—the union of the Americas—which has been alive in
the hemisphere ever since its nations won their independence.

It describes also a specific group of people, the multinational work force which constitutes the General
Secretariat of the Organization of American States.

This Pan American Secretariat is headquartered in an
edifice which, because of the rich symbolism of its structure

*The patio
of the Pan
American Union*

and interiors, has become one of the famous sites of the New World.

A brilliant ensign whips in the brisk winds on the top terrace of the building. This silken standard, composed of the flags of the twenty-one American nations in their natural colors, on a white disk in a blue field, is the banner of the Organization of American States.

This organization is the structure supporting the idea of Pan American union. It is the core of a network of multi-national agreements and arrangements in the Americas which reach back in time over a century and a half and forward in hope to a united hemisphere.

A visitor entering the building finds himself enveloped

at once in a milky light which draws him to the heart of the house. There a formal tropical patio sends exotic whispers and fragrances into the rain-forest air. Under the protective cover of a thick, translucent roof, date and jipijapa palms rustle languorously, rubber and coffee trees glow, and the pungent yerba maté tea plant haunts the nostrils. Black mosaic Aztec warriors, Inca princes, and Mayan nobles look up from the pink marble walks. In the center a fountain splashes slowly into its rose-colored basin decorated with eight feathered serpents and a Mexican star.

Across the patio, in the section just beyond the nodding palms, is a corridor with an audiovisual display of the Alliance for Progress. This joint U.S. - Latin American effort to bring material advance and social justice to all of the hemisphere, the Alliance for Progress, has been called an American partnership in the reach for new horizons. A Pan American gallery of paintings and sculptures opening off the Alliance for Progress exhibit presents an artistic vision of that reach.

Following the Alliance corridor to its end brings the visitor to the Pan American bookshop. Turning the corner there, one passes a treasure trove, the gift shop of the Americas. Then the colorful corridor changes abruptly as it becomes the hallway of the O.A.S. Department of Public Information, with its rushed rabbit-hutch offices, the steady stutter of typewriters, and the rhythmic reports of news tickers clattering the day's happenings in the hemisphere.

These streamlined sounds are pierced every so often by the primordial screech of a macaw. Two parrots live in the jungle square at the heart of the building, their garish plumes glistening in the patio's foliage like iridescent balloons.

The macaws' screams have been known to puncture mellifluous oratory in the paneled chamber of the O.A.S. Council where sleek armchairs are equipped with earphones for simultaneous translation in the organization's four official languages: English, Spanish, Portuguese, and French.

A small, almost secret door leads from this council room to the delegates' lounge, an intimate room of low lights and low tables where oratory simmers down to conversation and public passions are converted into continental compromises.

There is another council room on the building's second floor, in the corner between the Hall of the Americas and

One of the macaws

the suite of offices from which the O.A.S. Secretary-General supervises and serves the hemisphere.

It is known as the Old Council Room. Its "round" table is a massive oval hewed from one mahogany giant of the Dominican Republic. Thronelike armchairs, also mahogany, are carved in the traditional Spanish fashion, with curved claws rounding off legs and arms, and the back of each chair bears the crest of an American nation. One of the chairs has never yet been used. It carries the coat of arms of Canada.

The Hall of the Americas, adjoining the Old Council Room, is the showpiece of the house.

It is considered by many the most beautiful room in Washington. It has classic proportions, twenty-four Corinthian columns, and enormous Tiffany chandeliers. Gold, white, and crystal, it serves as glamorous setting for Pan American festivity.

This fantastic building, clutching the subsoil of Washington with symbolic roots of peace, guarded by emblems

Xochipili, god of flowers, in the garden of the House of the Americas. The Washington Monument is seen in the background.

of liberty and man's mastery of the globe, with an ancient Indian god meditating on water lilies in a park which borders Constitution Avenue, is the House of the Americas: blend of South American vision and imagination, beauty and mystery, with the purpose and substance, progress and solidity of the North; amalgam of the New World's two continents, their nature and history; mixture of the cultures these continents produced, and expression of the dream they share.

Of this house Elihu Root, first U.S. Secretary of State to win the Nobel Peace Prize, said on May 11, 1908, when its cornerstone was laid:

"Temples of religion, of patriotism, of learning, of art, of justice, abound; but this structure will stand alone, the first of its kind—a temple dedicated to international friendship."

And in this house U.S. Vice-President Hubert Humphrey, addressing an audience of Latin American diplomats on Pan American Day, 1965, declared:

"We are friends; we are partners; we are good neighbors. . . .

"Our doubt of today is the only limit to the realization of our dream of tomorrow."

President Theodore Roosevelt at Pan American Union
cornerstone ceremonies in 1908

BOLÍVAR'S
DREAM

The dream was Bolívar's. A hundred and fifty years ago he foresaw a continental community, foretold a hemisphere without frontiers.

Simón Bolívar was born in 1783, in the city of Caracas, a metropolis exceeding at the time the populations of Boston, Philadelphia, Baltimore, Charleston, or New York.

Among the earliest Spanish settlers in South America, the Bolívars had already raised three generations in the New World before the *Mayflower* set sail. The Crown of Castile had granted them a vast estate of virgin lands which they turned into a plantation, using native Indian and imported Negro labor. Young Simón spent most of his childhood on the family *hacienda* in San Mateo, with Indian and Negro boys as his playmates. They taught him to hunt, fish, and ride before he was eight years old. More important, they taught him ingenuity and physical endurance, the fusion of body and will which later helped to make him one of the greatest military leaders the Americas have produced.

Simón Bolívar

When Bolívar was three years old his father died. Young Simón's education was entrusted to his uncle, who discharged his duty by engaging for the boy private tutors to introduce him to the traditional worlds of art, science, and the humanities. Much of what these tutors imparted had a cobwebby quality for which young Simón had no patience. He ignored his teachers and the rote learning they asked of him as much as he could and read, hungrily and widely, on his own.

What interested him was how knowledge could be made to serve man—now.

When Simón was seventeen, his uncle suggested that he go to Europe for what was then a gentleman's mandatory grand tour of France, Italy, and Spain.

Bolívar, attracted by the adventure of encountering other

peoples and their ideas, readily agreed. His first destina-
tion was Madrid and he arrived in the Spanish capital with
introductions to many of its great houses as well as to the
court. He was, at first, very well received. He was elegant,
educated, of a good family—and rich. His annual income
at the age of eighteen was the equivalent of $100,000 a year.

But the attraction between the Old World and young
Bolívar was, and remained, a one-sided affair. Bolívar was
bored by the endless petty intrigues percolating through
the Spanish court, felt stifled in the rigid hierarchies of
Spanish life. He was unhappy with the political tyranny he
saw around him and disgusted by what seemed to his egali-
tarian American spirit a lack of dignity in the relationship
between men.

The one exception to his dislike of the Old World was
fifteen-year-old María Teresa de Toros, with whom he fell
in love. Two years his junior, María Teresa was a delicate,
spirited girl unhappy in the medievally fashionable cage of
her home. Bolívar courted her impetuously and ardently,
until her father forbade him the house for a year. He was
back the day that year was over, his mind and heart un-
changed. They were married a few weeks later, with young
Simón determined to take his wife home immediately to
the free air and wide spaces of America. They set sail for
Venezuela, but ten months later María Teresa was dead of
yellow fever, not yet seventeen. Bolívar never married
again.

Having buried his wife in America, he returned to Europe, this time to France, and once again the rich and
elegant young man from Caracas was in demand. Shortly
after Bolívar arrived in Paris, Napoleon was about to have

himself crowned emperor and young Bolívar received an invitation to attend Napoleon's coronation. But when the crested envelope came he threw it into the wastebasket, declaring that he had no wish to be witness to another tyrant in the making.

Deeply disappointed by the decay and disuse into which the great ideals of the French Revolution had fallen so quickly, he left France for Rome.

There the Spanish ambassador took him to the Vatican to present him to the Pope. It was the custom in those days for visitors to kneel before the Holy Father and brush his foot with their lips. Bolívar refused. It was an undignified position, he said, for one man to assume toward another.

Only one sight in Europe moved him. There is a hill in Rome from which one can see the entire city: Forum and Colosseum, pines and fountains. What young Bolívar remembered, looking down at the ancient capital, was that the mountain on which he stood had been the scene of the Roman people's revolt against their foreign rulers, the spot where they had demanded, and won, their first political rights. The date of that revolt was 494 B.C.

Was it not time for the people of South America to do as much?

Bolívar's answer to the question that seized his imagination in Rome was yes, an urgent yes. He devoted the rest of his life to the endeavor.

In South America the fight for independence began in 1810 and lasted a decade and a half. It was a more desperate struggle than the one in North America had been, and a harder one.

Politically, Spain was more unyielding than Britain,

medieval in both her thinking and her methods. Spain considered negotiations with her colonies an offense to her pride, and her way of dealing with political opponents was to starve them to death in the dungeons of fortresses with which she had barbed the landscape of the New World as well as the Old.

More intense in ferocity, the fight for freedom in South America was larger in scope as well. While the United States became independent with a population of less than 4,000,000, in South America more than 20,000,000 persons were chafing under colonial rule. They lived and fought in an area fifty times the size of that occupied by England's thirteen colonies in North America. In South America the clamor for independence rang from Cartagena on the Caribbean coast to the frozen tip of Cape Horn, and from Buenos Aires on the Atlantic Ocean to Guayaquil guarding the Pacific. Campaigns in Latin America's war of independence were fought in steaming jungles and on bare pampas, along verminous tropical shores and on the peaks of ice-crusted mountains 15,000 feet high.

Bolívar participated in most of them. At one point in the fifteen-year seesaw battle he led his army across the Andes, the roof of the Americas, higher and more exposed than the Rockies. Military experts rate this feat with Hannibal's crossing of the Alps. To the slim, almost frail man with the pale face and enormous deep-set eyes who, carefully barbered and dressed in silk shirts, could outride and outfight his toughest trooper, mastering the Andes was just one more conquest in a war which simply could not be lost.

Like Thomas Paine, Bolívar believed freedom to be a value in itself, a supreme value without which nothing of worth could be accomplished, while with it every achievement was open to man.

And so they won. Spain finally surrendered after her defeat in the battle of Ayacucho, on December 9, 1824. From that day on Bolívar dedicated all he had left of health, energy, and possessions to the campaign for what he considered to be clear corollaries to independence in America: constitutional government and a united hemisphere.

In both undertakings he faced staggering odds. Spain had permitted not an iota of self-government in her colonies. In administration, in trade, in transportation, as well as in every aspect of personal life—from ladies' fashions to religious ritual—Spain had tied her possessions to Madrid. When the people of Hispano America finally fought free, they found themselves heirs to the devastation and demoralization of a fifteen-year war. The emerging nations had had no experience in civil government, their economies were built on exclusive exchange with Spain, and they had neither understanding of nor communication with each other. The only patrimony they received was a chaotic continent.

The United States at that time was coping with continental chores of her own: expansion, consolidation, making the melting pot work. She wanted only to be left alone. During the entire war of independence in Latin America the United States remained strictly neutral. Only when there seemed to be a possibility that the reactionary powers of Europe, united in what they chose to call the Holy Alliance, might come to the aid of Spain in America did the United States act.

The action took the form of the Monroe Doctrine, a

President James Monroe established the principles of the Monroe Doctrine

unilateral statement by President James Monroe that he would consider any attempt by a European power to re-entrench itself in the New World as an act unfriendly to the United States. President Monroe never consulted with the leaders of Latin America. Nor was his declaration ratified by the United States Congress. It was his personal "hands off" warning to Europe. But it was backed by a grass-root feeling that swayed the Americas from pole to pole. And Europe took heed.

Perhaps Bolívar was aware of the same mute consensus when he called the first Pan American Congress, in Panama, in the summer of 1826. The last Spanish flag in the New World had been hauled down at the fortress of Real Felipe, in Callao, Peru, on January 23 of that year. On June 22, at the driving insistence of Bolívar, the first

Pan American Congress met to discuss the future of the hemisphere.

Bolívar knew exactly what he wanted that future to be and had designed the tools to shape it.

He saw America as *"el continente de palabras* [the continent of words]," where men would settle their differences by discussion and solve their problems by the processes of reason.

One hundred and forty years later President Lyndon B. Johnson was to express the same sentiment, using the biblical formulation, "Come now and let us reason together."

Bolívar knew that such reasoning would have to be grounded in shared assumptions and applied by equitable methods.

He visualized a Pan American league in which all the states of the New World would be united under a common international law, based on the proposition that nations, as well as men, are created equal.

Within the league, mediation and arbitration would serve to solve problems, dissolve disputes. The same tools of reason would be applied to conflicts arising between any member of the league and an outside power. If, however, such an outside power proved unamenable to peaceful settlement, or if a member of the league was threatened with anarchy from within, the entire league would lend immediate support to the threatened nation. For such eventualities, Bolívar proposed that the league maintain both an army and a navy.

This idea, too, materialized a hundred and forty years later when the Organization of American States formed the

Inter-American Peace Force to settle, in the Dominican Republic, a problem partaking of both dangers foreseen by Bolívar: internal anarchy and the threat of external aggression.

As an expression of political vision, the first Pan American Congress was, in Bolívar's own prophetic words, "immortal in the history of America."

As practical politics, it was a failure.

Only Colombia, Peru, Central America, and Mexico sent full delegations, of two plenipotentiaries each. No one came from Chile. Bolivia could not make up its mind. Río de la Plata, the territory now known as the Argentine, abstained on all decisions, as did Brazil. The United States dawdled disinterestedly when the call came, finally dispatched two men. One of these, the U.S. ambassador to Bogotá, died of yellow fever on the way. The other, traveling from Washington, arrived in Panama after the Congress had adjourned. In any case, neither had been given any power to act.

Physically, the delegates who did attend the Congress were wretched. Bolívar had chosen Panama as the site for the meeting because it was located at the mid-point of the hemisphere and constituted as well a narrow bridge connecting Pacific and Atlantic, the two major oceans girding both Americas. But Panama then, as now, was sodden with heat and humidity, and tropical diseases were rampant.

For three weeks the delegates labored in dispiriting discomfort. Then they decided to adjourn the Congress to the more hospitable climate of Mexico, at a later date.

The next time a major Pan American meeting took place

in Mexico was in 1901, three quarters of a century after the Congress of Panama.

The last years of Bolívar's personal life were as disappointing as had been the public events at Panama. While the people of his country and continent remembered and hailed him as their liberator, men of ambition and greed plotted his assassination. He escaped one such attempt, planned for execution at a gala ball presumably given in his honor, by climbing out of a back window during a pause in the dancing and spending the night hiding under a bridge in his gold-embroidered dress coat.

He finally decided to quit the contentions boiling around him and live out his days in self-imposed exile. He was on his way to Europe, but neither his funds nor his health held out long enough to get him there. He stopped to rest at a friend's estate in the port city of Santa Marta on the Colombian coast. He was never able to leave it. Tuberculosis was the physical cause of death, but the ship's doctor from a U.S. man-of-war in port, who tended Bolívar during his last hours, reported that the patient had no longer any desire to live. He was only forty-seven years old when he died.

To a former fellow fighter who had come to see him at Santa Marta a few weeks earlier, Bolívar had said: "Those of us who have toiled for the liberty of America have but plowed the sea."

For the sixty years following, it seemed as if Bolívar's despairing comment at death, rather than his life and vision, would become the truth for America.

The continent he had led to independence fell into a state

of confusion and turmoil which seemed to combine all the social and economic atrophy introduced by Spain with the divisive drive of raw nationalisms. For a while it looked as if the countries of Latin America were getting the worst of both worlds.

One attitude they inherited from Spain was disdain for the northern half of the hemisphere.

When the two American continents were first discovered and explored, the north held little to interest a conquistador. The native population was small—less than 1,000,000 Indians on the entire continent, and most of these roving, hunting, primitive tribes. South America, by contrast, had sizable Indian communities—the estimate was 12,000,000 —organized in splendid and wealthy civilizations. As the conquistadors saw it, Aztecs, Mayas, and Incas had treasures worth acquiring.

Also, as far as the Spaniards could tell at the time, North America had neither gold nor silver, and these were Spain's main interests in the New World. Madrid called the American lands it had been fortunate and brave enough to find and conquer the *dorados* (the gold lands), and considered the north a wilderness where neither nature nor man had anything to interest or concern a civilized Spaniard.

The heirs of Spain's Golden Age believed in addition that Latins in general, and Spaniards in particular, were the direct descendants of the classic triumphs of Greece and Rome, in culture and character the paragons of Western civilizations. They tended to regard the peoples of the north as barbarians, savage and cold, and Anglo-Saxons specifically as devoted to materialism, trade, and generally vulgar values.

*Delegates to the first Pan American Conference
in Washington, D.C., 1889–1890*

For three centuries North America was dismissed by the south on all grounds as "the land of no importance whatsoever."

The ignorance and arrogance worked both ways. When the first Pan American Congress met at Panama, not a single Spanish dictionary existed in the United States. And the failure of the Congress was shrugged off by President John Quincy Adams with the comment:

"As to an American system, we have it; we constitute the whole of it."

But the ghost of Bolívar could not be laid to rest. It was too insistent and made too much sense.

In the south, the Latin American countries continued, intermittently and haphazardly, to discuss unity, alliance, confederation, co-operation of some kind. In the United States, by 1880, Congress had begun to believe that an intercontinental get-together was perhaps not such a bad idea after all. Between 1880 and 1889, Congress passed a number of resolutions to that effect. In the fall of 1889, Secretary of State James G. Blaine followed through on the near decade of congressional prodding and invited all American states to send delegates to a meeting in Washington to discuss "peace, commerce, and mutual prosperity."

They came. Eighteen of the nineteen Latin American nations then in existence participated in talks which lasted six and a half months.

Secretary Blaine was a practical man, inclined to think that seeing is believing and that face-to-face talk around a table is likely to produce results. Before the delegates settled down to work in Washington he sent them on a 6000-mile trip through the United States in a luxurious special railway. In the course of that journey the Latin American delegates made two important discoveries. First, that, whatever the north might have been in the past, it was certainly no longer a land of no importance. And, second, that they were made welcome wherever they went, not only by officials but by workers who waved caps at them as they traveled through the cities and by farmers who hailed them with pitchforks and scythes as their Pullman passed through the countryside.

Back in Washington, the delegates discussed a number of projects, agreed on one fundamental principle, and took one concrete action. Among the projects they explored were reciprocal trade agreements, a hemispheric customs union, and the establishment of an inter-American bank.

The principle upon which they agreed declared that, regardless of the way the rest of the world felt on the issue, or had felt in the past, the American states were convinced that war was no solution to problems between them. They agreed to substitute arbitration.

The concrete result of the conference was the establishment, on April 14, 1890, of the Commercial Bureau of the American Republics. The Bureau was to gather data on the possibilities of trade among the American nations and make available to all interested parties the facts collected.

The Commercial Bureau of the American Republics: not a very inspiring name and, it seemed to many, both in America and in a scoffing Europe, not a very ambitious undertaking. But on this bare basis was built over the years a structure of practical hemispheric co-operation in matters ranging from mosquito control to the peaceful uses of nuclear energy, from the propagation of literacy to the organization of defense against subversive terror.

By mid-1890, then, the symbolic House of the Americas had a roof designed in Panama and a foundation laid in Washington. The task remaining was to build the walls which would join the two.

Building these walls turned out to be a demanding, laborious job that has not been finished yet.

The period following the Washington conference was a difficult one for Latin America and a demanding one for the United States. Once again the continents seemed to be heading in opposite directions. Latin America retreated further into political chaos, economic sluggishness, and provincial pettiness. The United States expanded, explosively and sometimes rapaciously.

When the United States bought Louisiana from Napoleon in 1803, and Alaska from the Russians in 1867, Latin American patriots approved. The purchases got Europe out of the Americas. But when the United States annexed Texas in 1845, and took a mammoth bite out of Mexico in the war that followed, wariness set in. The wariness changed to suspicion when the United States took over Puerto Rico after the war with Spain in 1889 and, for three years after that war was over, ran Cuba by means of a military occupation.

Suspicion turned into active resentment as private and public adventures led to U.S. interference in the affairs of Nicaragua, Haiti, the Dominican Republic, and, once again, Cuba.

South America was shocked by U.S. Secretary of State Richard Olney's blunt, tactless—and accurate—assertion, just before the turn of the century, that "the United States is practically sovereign in this continent; its fiat is law." Latin Americans were haunted by the then prevalent U.S. notion of "manifest destiny" which in a few decades had turned a struggling, searching, coalescing collection of states into the monolithic "Colossus of the North."

When Porfirio Díaz, dictator of Mexico until 1911, made his still famous comment on the relationship between his own country and the United States, his voice found an echo in all Latin America.

"Poor Mexico," Díaz said, "so far from God and so close to the United States. . . ."

By the early 1930s, U.S.-Latin American relations had sunk into a murky, slippery morass.

Fortunately for both Americas, President Franklin

President Franklin D. Roosevelt witnesses signing of reciprocal tariff treaty between the United States and Brazil, February 1935

Delano Roosevelt succeeded in draining the swamp. President Roosevelt set out to convince South America that what the United States really wanted was to be a good neighbor. The first step President Roosevelt took to demonstrate this attitude was to send Secretary of State Cordell Hull to Montevideo, Uruguay, in 1933 to sign the Convention on the Rights and Duties of American States. The key clause in that convention affirms that "no state has the right to intervene in the internal or external affairs of another."

Following through on this commitment, President Roosevelt withdrew all U.S. military forces from Latin America and put an end as well to northern political and economic pressures. In less than a decade he restored relations between the Americas to a new high of trust and co-operation.

F.D.R.'s Good Neighbor Policy turned out to be a valuable investment. When Japan attacked Pearl Harbor and the Axis began to aim its submarines and subversion at the American continents, it met a united hemisphere. The Good Neighbor Policy had turned the Monroe Doctrine into a Pan American commitment.

The commitment was formalized at Chapultepec Castle in Mexico City early in 1945, at the Inter-American Conference on Problems of War and Peace, in a set of resolutions called the Act of Chapultepec. That Act in turn was incorporated into the Inter-American Treaty of Reciprocal Assistance, signed in Rio de Janeiro in 1947 and known as the Rio Treaty. Abjuring war once again, and committing its signators to methods of peaceful settlement in controversies between them, the Rio Treaty bears witness to its Bolivarian inspiration, and makes clear its Pan American character, by declaring that "an armed attack by any State against an American State shall be considered as an attack against all the American States."

Moving from the Rio Treaty to the creation of the Organization of American States, to implement the resolutions for co-operation in war and peace, was a logical, short and quick step.

The Rio Treaty was completed on September 2, 1947. On March 30, 1948, the American states met in Bogotá, Colombia, and in just over four weeks wrote the Charter of the O.A.S.

The O.A.S. Charter is an impressive document. It is not

*Secretary of State Marshall (center) in Bogotá, Columbia
where charter of the O.A.S. was written*

just a practical accommodation like Britain's Magna Carta. Nor is it primarily an ideological manifesto such as the document the French Revolution produced. Neither is it simply a balanced statement of rights and obligations and the processes required to secure them, as is the Constitution of the United States.

The O.A.S. Charter is all of these and more. It is pragmatic in the most profound sense of the word, taking cognizance that man is shaped by his philosophy as well as his practice, his ideas as much as his institutions.

In 112 paragraphs the O.A.S. Charter gathers up the full range of the hemisphere's experience of yesteryears and America's aspiration for the future.

Both of these—experience and aspiration—says the

O.A.S. Charter in its preamble, derive from "America's historic mission: to offer to man a land of liberty...."

Bolívar could have asked no more.

The next move was to make the Charter work.

HOW
THE O.A.S.
WORKS

"When extremes of climate meet, they produce tornadoes."

This wry observation, intended to describe the contemporary political atmosphere of the Americas, was made by Dr. José A. Mora, third Secretary-General of the Organization of American States, whose face bears the marks of the international storms he has weathered.

Colombia's Alberto Lleras Camargo piloted the O.A.S. through its first three turbulent years. He was followed by Chile's Carlos Dávila, a veteran advocate of Pan Americanism, under whose aegis the Organization began to steer a still stormy but somewhat steadier course.

Uruguay's Dr. Mora took over in 1958 and will be the only O.A.S. Secretary-General to serve a ten-year term. At the Second Special Inter-American Conference in Rio de Janeiro, Brazil, in November 1965, it was decided to limit all future Secretaries-General to five-year periods of service. Dr. Mora headed the Organization during its

Dr. José A. Mora, third Secretary-General of the O.A.S.

brightest moments, when the Alliance for Progress was born, and during its darkest hours, when the discovery of Soviet atomic missiles in Cuba blackened the hemispheric horizon.

"In nature," Dr. Mora has observed, "when a mass of hot air comes upon a concentration of cold air, the shock produces a storm. The same law operates in politics.

"When a very rich, highly industrialized, materially advanced nation comes into contact with a poor, stagnant, underdeveloped area, a clash results on impact.

"When a politically mature people finds itself dealing with a society rutted in narrow old furrows, sparks are inevitably struck."

That lightning should flash across the American skies, with their very wide spectrum of political and economic climate, seems to Dr. Mora only natural. To his mind, the important fact is that the time is past when everyone talked about the weather but no one did anything about it.

He is concerned with the realization that we know enough about the political atmosphere to be able to prepare for storms and be safe. We can even head off some tempests, he believes, so they will blow harmlessly out to sea. Most important, Dr. Mora holds we can work toward preventing storms altogether by modifying the extremes of political and economic climate in the hemisphere.

And in his view this control of "climate" and prevention of storms is the basic task of the O.A.S.

It is only reasonable that such a complex and delicate undertaking should require complex and delicate machinery: big radar screens to catch the sounds and echos of the hemisphere; and small, sharply tooled precision instruments to measure and adjust the sometimes minute flaws and discrepancies which make the difference between painful and risky abrasions and a system that functions smoothly.

A chart of the instruments devised to date by the O.A.S. is on page 40.

Topping the chart's vertical axis is the Inter-American Conference, the supreme policy-making body of the Pan American idea. Bolívar's Congress at Panama in 1826 was its precursor. The assembly called by Secretary of State Blaine in Washington in 1889 was its first session. Its meetings are irregular. Decades have elapsed between conferences, but there have been times also when hemisphere needs required an exchange of views and the formulation of policies at top level every other year, or even annually. Inter-American Conferences are attended by the hemispheres's most important men. They are the summit of the system.

The center circle on the chart's vertical axis—and the hub of the chart—is the Council of the O.A.S. It operates as the executive committee of the system. All member nations are represented on it, by delegates of equal rank and

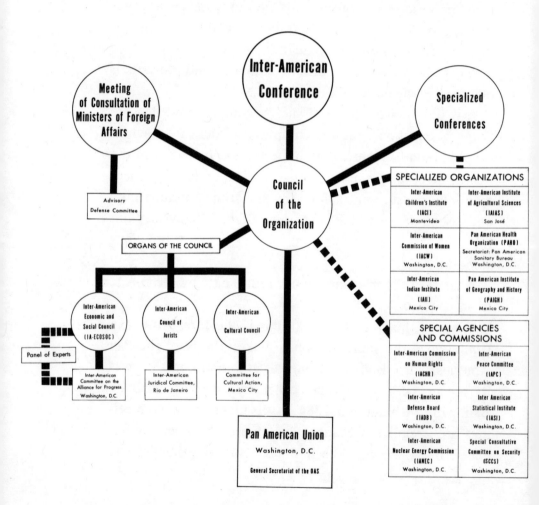

with an equal voice and vote. Each delegate is a fully accredited ambassador extraordinary and plenipotentiary. Whether he represents one of the giants in the American system—the United States with its 200,000,000 people, Brazil with 80,000,000, Mexico with 40,000,000, Argentina with 22,000,000—or its tiniest member—Costa Rica with 1,400,000—the delegate casts the same one vote in the Council's deliberations. And there is no veto.

Since the system is very much a going concern, the O.A.S. Council is in permanent session. Its ambassadorial delegates meet regularly on the first and third Wednesdays of each month, plus any other day of the week, or hour of the day, if developments call for extraordinary sessions. Weary Council delegates, perusing their papers and telegrams, arguing stresses and strains, have seen dawn come up over Washington many a time following emergency sessions that lasted through the night.

The Council's meetings are held in Washington, in the Council's chamber in the House of the Americas. The Council elects its own chairman and vice-chairman each year. To make certain that every country gets its turn at the helm, neither the chairman nor the vice-chairman is eligible for re-election.

The Council's priority assignment is to execute the policies laid down by the Inter-American Conferences. The Council also takes orders from the Meetings of Consultation of Foreign Ministers. The Foreign Ministers of the Americas meet when issues require consultation on a high level but not quite high enough to call out the top leaders of the hemisphere. The Foreign Ministers take advice from the O.A.S. Council, as well as give it instructions.

Another Council task is to co-ordinate the activities of its own organs and of the network of special conferences, organizations, agencies, and committees connected with it by a variety of arrangements.

Finally, the Council supervises the activities of the Pan American Union, the 1200-member Secretariat of the O.A.S.

The men and women who make up that Secretariat are an extraordinary team. They hail from skyscraper cities and tropical islands, from treeless pampas and rain-forest jungles, from tin-roof slums and mountain log cabins. They range the full palette of human color and constitute a prism of backgrounds and traditions.

Yet they are all Americans. Someone once observed that you can always tell an American by his walk. His stride is long, his stance loose. He comes from a society which is open, a continent with large spaces, a hemisphere that stretches to the horizon.

At the Pan American Union you can see how accurate this observation is. Whatever his individual size or stature, every member of the O.A.S. Secretariat has something of that large and easy American stride.

They also have the characteristically American approach of expecting direct contact with the chief, when an issue or situation warrants it. The Pan American Union is probably the only international organization whose staff members requested a personal briefing from the boss, just returned from grappling with a crisis, and received an immediate response.

When O.A.S. Secretary-General Mora came back to Washington from the Dominican Republic early in June

1965, after his six-week effort at personal peacemaking, the O.A.S. Secretariat asked that he meet with the staff and report just what he had encountered and done. The meeting took place within forty-eight hours after Dr. Mora's return. The staff listened, asked questions, practically grilled the Secretary-General. When he had given his account, replied to all queries, responded to all barbs, and fended off every heckler, the members of the Pan American Union gave him an ovation—and went back to work.

The Pan American Union's work consists of serving and servicing every one of the instrumentalities which make up the O.A.S. It is the P.A.U.'s responsibility to keep O.A.S. machinery well oiled, in good repair, and in a serviceable state.

Three major pieces of equipment in the Secretariat's care are the special organs of the O.A.S. Council: the Inter-American Economic and Social Council; the Inter-American Council of Jurists; and the Inter-American Cultural Council, which at the end of 1965 was renamed the Inter-American Educational, Scientific, and Cultural Council.

The members of this important O.A.S. triumvirate are accurately named.

The concern of the Inter-American Economic and Social Council, with its bouncing abbreviation IA-ECOSOC, is "the promotion of the economic and social welfare of the American nations."

That, of course, is a tall order and IA-ECOSOC is one of the major pillars sustaining the O.A.S. Its interests and activities range from bananas to ports, from the encouragement of rural co-operatives to the modernization of city planning, from the marketing of coffee to the construction of the Pan American Highway. Any undertaking, any method that promotes the better utilization of America's natural resources, any effort that contributes to the development of agriculture or industry, any idea or project that helps to raise living standards in the hemisphere falls within the comprehensive jurisdiction of IA-ECOSOC.

Under its aegis the American peoples conceived, planned, and put into operation the Alliance for Progress, a new concept of international co-operation in the field of economic development and social growth.

To make certain that there will be a corps of experts to backstop IA-ECOSOC, to spark and activate continued economic and social progress, the O.A.S. awards about 2500 fellowships each year to advanced students. These scholarships are for training, research, or specialized study, with particular emphasis on economics, public and business administration, agriculture, architecture, city planning, statistics, engineering, industrial technology, veterinary medicine, geology, mining, physics, and chemistry. O.A.S. fellows pledge themselves to go home, after they have acquired the needed knowledge, to help turn the ideas and plans of IA-ECOSOC into reality.

Lined up alongside IA-ECOSOC in the chart of the Organization, and operating in the same relationship to the system, is the Inter-American Council of Jurists.

No informal initials exist for this Council, the legal brain, and sometimes the legal arm, of the O.A.S. Its assignment is to develop and codify public and private law in the Americas. Whenever and wherever desirable and possible, the

Council of Jurists also endeavors to standardize law for the American nations. Thus it breaks ground for a continental community founded on the security of law rather than the caprices of men.

In some areas hemispheric law already exists. It covers such particular problems as salvage at sea and tackles such taut issues as the right of asylum. Hemispheric law is being written now in comparatively minor but indicative matters like the protection of copyright; the weightier concerns of commercial arbitration, extradition of criminals, agricultural and industrial use of international rivers and lakes; and the very major complex of codes which, when completed, will constitute a Convention on Human Rights with an Inter-American Court of Human Rights to see to it that individual justice is done in the hemisphere.

The third in the row of Council organs shown on the chart is the Inter-American Cultural Council. Its fascinating task is "to facilitate and promote cultural, scientific, and educational exchange between the nations of the Americas."

It has arranged book fairs and established libraries, organized concerts and artistic exhibitions. It has promoted meetings and exchanges of American philosophers and men of letters, composers, painters, and experts in the social as well as the natural sciences. The Inter-American Cultural Council is a permanent clearinghouse for the creative ideas and works of the hemisphere.

In recent years it has added a new concern to its range of activities: culture on the most basic level, the eradication of illiteracy from the American landscape.

Millions of American adults today can neither read nor write and an equal number of American children have never seen the inside, or even the outside, of a school.

Over-all illiteracy in the Americas is still a shocking 50% ranging from Uruguay's 5% to Haiti's 90%. The Inter-American Cultural Council has faced the fact that, just as a political democracy is no stronger than its weakest link, so no culture is ever more truly flourishing than the grass-roots foundation from which it draws its nourishment.

The Cultural Council has therefore made education its primary preoccupation. It is concentrating its energies now on the improvement of school systems and their administration, on a more appropriate curriculum that will provide for Latin America fewer lawyers and more veterinarians, fewer philosophers and more agronomists.

The Cultural Council concerns itself also with better training for teachers; the most efficient and inexpensive way to build schools; literacy programs for adults; and, finally, the development of uniform educational standards for the entire hemisphere, so that in the future students of every age and scholars of every field can go anywhere in the Americas and find their proper place.

The circular system of Councils on the one side of the O.A.S. chart is balanced on the other side by a double series of oblongs, each representing an organization, agency, or commission connected with the system.

The first of these oblongs—and indeed the first in importance for America's future—is the Inter-American Children's Institute.

Many children in the Americas, particularly in South

America, have very real problems. They begin at birth. In some Latin American countries infant mortality is still distressingly high: as many as fifty children in every thousand never reach their first birthday. Children who survive this hazardous first year of life often have their health undermined by malnutrition in the decade following. A serious lack of proteins, the result of inadequate diet or bad nutritional education of parents, has produced throughout Latin America the stunted child with his swollen belly whose attention span is so short that he cannot absorb even the alphabet in school; who frequently lands in a hospital for months at a time; and who often dies before he reaches teen age.

Child Welfare Institute in Port-au-Prince, Haiti

Nutrition centers help supplement the daily diet. This one is at Santa Catarina Barahona, Guatemala.

A large number of children in the hemisphere have legal and social problems as well. In Latin America particularly, a great many families have no legal basis and literally millions of children are abandoned by their fathers, their mothers, and sometimes both. Every newspaper in Latin America too often carries photographs showing a sad-eyed child or group of children staring, lost or accusing, from the printed page. Invariably the caption reads:

"Why have you left us?"

And, tragically, no one replies.

An inevitable result of this state of affairs is that as soon as such children get old enough to wonder, think, and resent they become restless, rootless, and rebellious.

It is the basic aim of the Inter-American Children's Institute to break this destructive and dangerous cycle and work toward a society which will "honor for all the children of the hemisphere the promise of America."

Women, too, still have their special problems in the hemisphere and their own organization, the Inter-American Commission of Women, to help find solutions.

Until 1920, not a single woman in the whole New World could cast a ballot. When the Inter-American Commission of Women was formed in 1928, only the United States had extended suffrage regardless of sex. In all of Latin America women could neither vote nor own property. If they wanted to travel they needed written permission from their husbands or legal guardians.

Winning full political rights for the female half of the hemisphere was the first goal the Inter-American Commission of Women set itself. It took more than thirty years to achieve. Not until 1961 did the last of the American nations, Paraguay, finally remove restrictions of sex from the ballot.

Concurrently with its struggle for suffrage, the Inter-American Commission of Women fought battles in allied areas. In 1933 it persuaded the American nations to eliminate discrimination in nationality. Until then a woman lost her own nationality if she married the citizen of another country. In many states women had no nationality of their own. They were the wards, as far as citizenship was concerned, of either their fathers or their husbands.

In 1948 the Commission of Women succeeded in pushing the American nations still another step forward on the

road to sex equality. It prepared, and persuaded governments to sign, a Convention on the Granting of Political
Rights to Women which entitles adults of both sexes not
only to vote but to hold public office.

Within fifteen years after that document was drawn Colombia had a woman in her Cabinet, Honduras had chosen
a lady as Minister of Labor, Nicaragua had appointed a
female Deputy Minister, and Guatemala a Secretary of
Social Welfare with Cabinet rank.

In addition, one Latin American nation had a woman on
its Supreme Court, a number had lady ambassadors, and a
sprinkling of women had begun to appear in legislatures
throughout the continent. By 1965 there was not a single
country in the hemisphere in which women were not, at
last, entering the professions and beginning to carve for
themselves prominent places in public life.

But the work of the Inter-American Commission of
Women is not yet done. Economic discrimination is still
prevalent throughout the hemisphere. Women tend to be
relegated to the lower-paying occupations, and "equal pay
for equal work" is a slogan not yet matched by the content
of wage envelopes.

Social barriers—all the unwritten, even unspoken, but
so compelling laws—also still operate to keep women in
purdahs of one kind or another.

Above all, the Inter-American Commission of Women
continues to experience the frustration of governments
agreeing with the Commission's proposals in public conferences—sometimes enthusiastically, sometimes merely
gallantly—and then going home and forgetting all about
their gentlemanly pledges. Too large a number of the con-

ventions drafted and the resolutions passed at the prompt-
ing of the Inter-American Commission of Women have
been quietly pigeonholed by some of the continents'
regimes.

But Commission leaders are hopeful. "There can be no
real development without America's women," they point
out. "Women constitute, after all, half of the hemisphere's
human resources. They will have to be used sooner or
later. And all indications are, in this new era of development dynamics, that it will be soon."

There is one other untapped human resource in the
Americas with a special O.A.S. agency to look after it. The
agency is the Inter-American Indian Institute and its mission is to bring the Indian peoples of the hemisphere into
the main stream of American life. A number of nations
still have substantial Indian populations either leading isolated, marginal existences on reservations, official or un-
official, or, more frequently, confined to their own secluded
and minimal lives. Sometimes these lives are peaceful but
haunted by poverty, disease, and superstition. More often
nowadays Indian populations are driven by the desperation
of their needs to social rebellion, and outright insurrection.

The Inter-American Indian Institute is designed to see
to it that every individual Indian gets his full legal, social,
and economic rights. At the same time the Institute strives
to preserve what remains of the ancient Indian civilizations,
and to add their valuable ingredients to the melting pot of
America. The Institute studies Indian customs and
concepts, traditions and languages, religions and social systems. It hopes to assure that these are woven into the cul-

tural fabric of the hemisphere, while sanitation and literacy, modern farming techniques and medical attention are brought to the Indian communities.

Members of the Organization of American States know that man does not live by bread alone, but the O.A.S. is conscious also of the fact that bread, in all its variations, is basic. The Inter-American Institute of Agricultural Sciences was created to make sure that the staff of life is both good and plentiful in the Americas.

The Institute takes an extensive view of its responsibilities. It conducts plant and animal research in both the Tropic and the Temperate Zones of the Americas. It spon-

School children in Grecia, Costa Rica, prepare to seed a vegetable garden

sors an institute for the study and development of agricultural credit and runs an Inter-American Center for Land
Reform. It promotes programs for the improvement of
rural life and has flung a network of information and service activities over the entire southern continent, directed
specifically at rural youth.

In Latin America vast areas of land and a substantial
segment of the population are dedicated to agriculture. The
production methods these sections of the continent em-
ploy, and the quality of the lives the people lead, are important factors in the happiness and prosperity of the
hemisphere.

How healthy the hemisphere will be is the business and
charge of the Pan American Health Organization, oldest of
the international agencies connected with the O.A.S.

During the more than half a century of its existence the
Pan American Health Organization has sent its DDT jeeps
into the remotest corners of the continent to wipe out ma-
laria; has practically eliminated yellow fever and smallpox;
is battling typhus and tuberculosis, leprosy and rabies; and
is straining every effort to eliminate the diarrheal diseases
which are still major killers, particularly of infants and
children, in Latin America.

The steady flow of experts, techniques, and information
employed in these tasks runs in many directions through
PAHO channels. A Brazilian expert, recruited through the
Health Organization, helped United States authorities in
their fight against the "Egyptian mosquito" which was
spreading yellow fever in Puerto Rico and the Virgin Islands as late as 1965. The Brazilian brought with him a

Cavalry tactics are used in an anti-malaria campaign in Mexico

yellow-fever vaccine from the Oswaldo Cruz Institute in Rio de Janeiro, which manufactures it for free distribution to all governments of the Americas.

In the past few years the Health Organization has widened its sphere of activity. PAHO experts have discovered that, just as a healthy mind needs a healthy body, a healthy body must have a sanitary environment.

In 1960 there were 110,000,000 persons in the American hemisphere without a safe supply of drinking water, and water-borne diseases were the leading cause of death in eight countries of Latin America.

In some parts of Latin America clean safe water is such a precious commodity that the government of one country brought water trucks to its slum population as a Christmas gift; in another country racketeers maneuvered, with violence and murder, to corner the water market.

The Pan American Health Organization launched a continent-wide campaign for clean water and sewage control in 1960. That year alone, 150,000 persons, mainly children, were killed by polluted water in Latin America.

Since 1960, PAHO engineers, water supply experts, and specialists on environmental health have fanned out over South America. At PAHO instigation, national water programs have been introduced in Bolivia, Costa Rica, El Salvador, Honduras, and Panama. In other Latin American nations, counties, cities, even villages have tackled the job

"Water day" comes three times a week to this village in Peru

*Villagers constructed water tank under guidance of an engineer
in Tovera, Guanajuato, Mexico*

on their own. The Inter-American Development Bank has
extended loans for major water and sewage installations
and, in some Indian villages, elders have collected pennies
from each householder to buy the pipe that will feed fresh
water to the community from a mountain spring or a newly
sunk well.

Between 1961 and 1963, PAHO persuaded the countries
of Latin America to invest a total of $321,000,000 in clean
water for their peoples.

The American continents have a number of other physical problems needing detailed and co-operative attention. One slice of Latin America, from Mexico on south past the equator, lies in what seismic terminology calls "the Pacific Fire Circle." Territories in that circle are jarred periodically by earthquakes and volcanic eruptions. Much havoc and tragedy have been caused over the years by these violent natural convulsions. Until recently, nothing could be done to safeguard man against them. Now, however, a new science exists: vulcanology, which not only probes the secrets of volcanic activity but is studying methods to convert the destructive energy, which for so long has harassed man from the core of the earth, to controlled energy which can be used to produce power and light.

Volcanic scientists of the New World pool their knowledge under the auspices of the Pan American Institute of Geography and History.

That O.A.S. agency also investigates America's earth, oceans, and air, its past and its future. Geology and cartography, geography and oceanology, geophysics and every facet of historical research are embraced in its far-roaming reach.

"The Pan American Institute of Geography and History," its president, Guatemala's Dr. Alfredo Obiols, has said, "is interested in American man, his environment, and the structure of his hemisphere.

"In this complete context, we want to know what we were and what we are, so that we can plan rationally what we want to be.

"Is this not the essence of Americanism?"

PEACE
AND
PROGRESS

During the height of the political crisis in the Dominican Republic in the late spring of 1965 the first sign of a possible peace appeared when a lone jeep with five men in it wove its exposed way through the narrow alleys of downtown Santo Domingo. The nose of the khaki-colored vehicle had a painted crest, a circle framing twenty-one flags: the seal of the Organization of American States.

The men in the jeep wore blue and gold arm bands with initials reading "O.E.A.," the abbreviation for the Spanish *Organización de los Estados Americanos.*

Wherever the jeep went the shooting stopped.

That O.A.S. peacemaking effort in the Dominican Republic—it proved to be a complex task involving a cease-fire, emergency financing and supplies, political negotiations, and the creation and first-time use of an Inter-American Peace Force—was only the most dramatic demonstration of the system's peace-keeping machinery at work.

The machinery, designed twenty-five years earlier and elaborated in 1947 and 1948, had been functioning quietly and successfully for close to two decades.

The problem of keeping the peace in the Americas had been a basic concern of all advocates of hemispheric co-operation from the very beginning. To Bolívar it had seemed that war was an obsolete instrument of policy for free and independent peoples. In addition, he considered its use un-American. One of his primary goals at the Pan-ama Congress was to have the delegates agree to outlaw war and commit themselves to the use of arbitration in any dispute that might arise between them.

At the first Inter-American Conference in Washington in 1890 the hemispheric delegates attending made that commitment officially.

But there was no device to enforce it or even to make it possible. Not until Hitler had demonstrated once again the horror and futility of a deliberate policy of violence did the Foreign Ministers of the Americas design a prac-tical instrument for peace-keeping. At a meeting in Havana in 1940 they voted to establish the Inter-American Peace Committee as a permanent autonomous organ "to insure that states between which any dispute or contro-versy exists will solve it as quickly as possible." And, of course, without resort to force.

The Rio Treaty of 1947 and the Pact of Bogotá, which was drawn to complement it the following year, reaffirm the obligation of all American states to settle disputes peacefully, and spell out in concrete detail every step of arbitration and conciliation available to parties in conflict. Both documents also alert the American states to the peace-keeping machinery at their disposal, including the Inter-American Peace Committee.

The new peace-keeping machinery proved its mettle that very same year, 1948, when Costa Rica came to the O.A.S. with the charge that it had been invaded by armed forces crossing its borders from Nicaragua.

A fact-finding committee dispatched to the spot confirmed the Costa Rican charges. Nicaragua, while prepared to support a little inexpensive political adventurism, was not willing to stand publicly condemned as an overt aggressor during that period of great inter-American amity. It withdrew its support of the invading forces and saw to it that the men involved returned to Nicaragua and disbanded—at least for the time being.

Pact between Costa Rica and Nicaragua went into effect in July 1949

All this was arranged officially but without fanfare under O.A.S. auspices, and sealed in a pact signed between Nicaragua and Costa Rica in February 1949. To permit a tactful retreat of the Nicaraguan invaders, the pact did not enter into force until mid-July, by which time the Nicaraguans had quietly faded away.

Nicaragua made another attempt of the same nature in 1955, when Costa Rica was governed in fine democratic fashion while Nicaragua was run by a dictator who would have preferred a more congenial regime next door.

Again, however, Costa Rica came to the O.A.S. The Organization acted within twenty-four hours—and Nicaragua decided, this time for good, that the game was not worth the candle. There has been no trouble between the two countries since. They are members of the Organization of Central American States, co-operate economically in the Central American Common Market, and work together successfully in finding solutions to concrete problems which concern them both: the building of a highway network which will facilitate travel and trade through the Central American isthmus, and the joint construction of hydroelectric facilities, using the water power of a river they share, and designed to serve customers on both sides of the border.

There have been times when the O.A.S. peace-keeping machinery merely had to be put into gear for a potential conflict to collapse. An instance of this was a wrangle between Haiti and the Dominican Republic in 1950, when each country charged the other with threatening its sovereignty and political independence. The O.A.S. sent to the site an investigating commission which found that these two close and crowded neighbors sharing an island were, in fact, meddling in each other's back yards. The O.A.S. referred both countries to the Inter-American Convention on the Duties and Rights of States in the Event of Civil Strife. In short, it asked them to behave. And for the following thirteen years they did.

Nor have countries assisted by O.A.S. peace-keeping machinery always been small members of the American family.

In January 1964, after incited groups of Panamanians had attacked U.S. personnel and property in the Canal Zone, the Inter-American Peace Committee rushed a delegation to the scene and managed to restrain the turbulent wave of resentment on both sides. Within days after the arrival of the peace group, public order had been restored and tempers had cooled to a point where reasonable talk became possible. Direct negotiations between Panama and the United States, held in Washington shortly after, went to the roots of the problem that had caused the outburst.

The O.A.S. had demonstrated earlier that its peace-keeping machinery could handle major problems.

In 1962, following the discovery of Soviet missiles in Cuba, the O.A.S. resolved immediately to do all in its power "to prevent the delivery of offensive weapons to Cuba and cause the withdrawal from Cuba, by the Soviet Union, of missiles and military personnel."

The Cuban missile menace, threatening as it was to the heartland of the Americas, alerted the O.A.S. to a new kind of danger: a threat to peace in the hemisphere from organized subversion within, directed, financed, and equipped from abroad.

Bolívar had visualized the possibility of aggression from abroad and the danger of anarchy from within; but even his imagination could not conjure the combination of the two which turned out to be the twentieth century's contribution to the ancient art of war.

As so often before, the inter-American system demonstrated its flexibility and ingenuity in facing up to this new challenge. It devised a new instrument, the Special Consultative Committee on Security, to "maintain all necessary vigilance to prevent acts of aggression, subversion, or other dangers to peace and security, or the preparation for such acts, resulting from the continued intervention of the Sino-Soviet powers in this hemisphere."

While it was coping with crises new and old, aggressions large and small, the O.A.S. never lost sight of the fact that the final meaning of peace and security is not the defense of any particular political system or economic structure, but the safety and freedom of the individual.

To secure these in the hemisphere, the O.A.S. created an Inter-American Commission on Human Rights, charged by its statutes with "promoting respect for human rights in the American Republics as embodied in the American Declaration of Rights and Duties of Man," the moral and philosophical bases on which the O.A.S. Charter rests.

That Declaration proclaims that "all men are born free and equal, in dignity and in rights and, being endowed by nature with reason and conscience, they should conduct themselves as brothers to one another."

It asserts also that "the fulfillment of duty by each individual is a prerequisite to the rights of all. Rights and duties are interrelated in every social and political activity of man. While rights exalt individual liberty, duties express the dignity of that liberty."

Members of the Inter-American Commission on Human Rights—there are seven—are not appointed by their governments, nor are they subject to the diplomatic niceties of area representation. They are elected by the O.A.S. Council, strictly on personal merit. What makes an American eligible to this Commission is his stature as a fighter for human dignity.

There is no area of contemporary human concern to which the Commission cannot address itself. It has dealt with passports for political refugees and with the dangers to individual freedom caused by protracted government-declared states of siege. It has applied its attention to the violation of voting rights in Alabama, the mistreatment of political prisoners in Cuba, the tensions set up, in the minds and hearts of their citizens, by undemocratic governments anywhere in the hemisphere.

The need for the Inter-American Commission on Human Rights, embodying the conscience of the hemisphere, became sadly evident in the Dominican Republic in 1965, when the Commission received reports of violations by both factions in the conflict, and hastened to the scene.

Unhappily, it found the reports to be only too true. Political prisoners had been put up against a wall and shot, with their hands tied behind their backs, by one side, and had been packed like sardines into foul-smelling prisons, on a starvation diet, by the other.

Commission revelations had the grim effect of shocking the hemisphere, and the salutary one of stopping the violations. Most important, they served as a warning to would-be perpetrators of similar offenses that, at least in the Americas, they would not get away with such crimes.

There was yet another kind of crime which the Organization of American States felt it could no longer allow.

Very soon after the Charter was written it became clear throughout the world that peace had begun to mean more than an absence of armed conflict. Everywhere, the freedoms from fear and want had become as compelling an urge as the freedoms of speech and religion. And of the four freedoms, in most instances freedom from want took the first priority. This was true even in the Americas where protests mounted that for far too many the way between *el hombre y el hambre* (man and hunger) had been lost and that something must be done quickly.

There was, in the late forties and early fifties, a general casting about by the countries of Latin America for a way to reconstitute their economies, which once again had begun to slow down or stall. There was also a groping for new social mechanisms that would propel these economies forward instead of freezing them in obsolete patterns.

It soon became evident that separate action by individual nations would achieve only too little, too late. The world, including the Americas, had become too small and interdependent for isolated effort to be effective. If the countries of Latin America were going to move and develop at the pace demanded by their peoples, and made possible by modern techniques and know-how, they would have to make a concentrated, concerted effort, and the United States would have to be an integral and committed participant in that effort.

Mr. Nelson Rockefeller gave the first formulation to this

idea when, early in the 1940s, he spoke of a Pan American economic union. In 1958, Brazilian President Juscelino Kubitschek amplified and dramatized the concept into a grand hemispheric design which, with appropriate emphasis on action, he called Operation Pan America.

Operation Pan America started with the assumption that hunger and need anywhere in the Americas were the concern of everyone in the Americas.

Just as the Americas had recognized a century earlier that the hemisphere could not long survive half slave and half free, so, President Kubitschek pointed out, it must recognize now that it cannot exist half rich and half poor.

Based on this conviction, Operation Pan America proceeded to take concrete steps.

It suggested the use, or adaptation for use, of existing inter-American institutions for an immediate onslaught on the problems of underdevelopment; the creation of new international financial institutions, or the expansion of existing ones, to furnish the financial tools for this undertaking; the harnessing of both private initiative and technical expertise; and finally, the planned, immediate revision of national policies to promote and push economic development at maximum speed.

The response by all the nations of the Americas to President Kubitschek's Operation was instantaneous. In September 1958 the Foreign Ministers of the Americas met in Washington and voted to establish a special Committee of 21 to devise ways and means to get Operation Pan America off the ground.

Early the following year agreement was reached on establishing the Inter-American Development Bank, an idea which had first been broached seventy years earlier but had lain dormant all this time.

In August 1960 the United States Congress authorized an appropriation of $500,000,000 for a special Inter-American Social Development Fund. It was the first major financial commitment the United States had made to Latin America since the end of World War II. To Latin America, the appropriation meant more than money. It indicated that, having helped Western Europe to pull itself out of the shambles of war, the United States felt free and ready at last to turn its attention to its own hemisphere.

A month after the U.S. Congress acted, the Committee of 21 met, once again in Bogotá, Colombia, to sign the Act of Bogotá, a comprehensive co-ordinated program to improve economic and social conditions in the hemisphere. The Council of the Organization of American States officially approved the Act on October 11, 1960, and it became the bedrock of economic policy in the hemisphere for the ensuing decade.

What were economic conditions in the Americas when the Committee of 21 drew up the Act of Bogotá?

The Committee found that 135,000,000 Americans were either undernourished, illiterate, poorly clothed, or living in unsanitary, makeshift dwellings, and earning between $50 and $300 a year. Two thirds of the people of Latin America were deprived in one or a combination of these ways, and even in the United States more than 7,000,000 persons were receiving some form of public assistance and almost 3,000,000 adults were illiterate.

Into this dark state of affairs a bright flare was sent by U.S. President John F. Kennedy.

On March 13, 1961, President Kennedy invited to the White House the Latin American diplomatic corps in Washington. There was little striped-pants chitchat at the meeting. President Kennedy spoke bluntly and with deep concern.

"Throughout Latin America—a continent rich in resources and in the spiritual and cultural achievements of its people," he said, "millions of men and women suffer the daily degradations of hunger and poverty. They lack decent shelter or protection from disease. Their children are deprived of the education or the jobs which are the gateway to a better life. And each day the problems grow more urgent. . . .

"If we are to meet a problem so staggering in its dimensions, our approach must itself be equally bold, an approach consistent with the majestic concept of Operation Pan America.

"I have therefore called on all the people of the hemisphere to join in a new Alliance for Progress—*Alianza para el Progreso*—a vast co-operative effort, unparalleled in magnitude and nobility of purpose, to satisfy the basic needs of the American people for homes, work and land, health and schools—*techo trabajo y tierra, salud y escuela. . . .*"

The Alliance for Progress had been conceived and proffered. In that same White House meeting President Kennedy spelled out what it could mean to the hemisphere.

"If we are successful," President Kennedy declared, "if our effort is bold enough and determined enough, then the close of this decade will mark the beginning of a new era in the American experience. The living standards of every

President John F. Kennedy signs the Alliance for Progress

family will be on the rise, basic education will be available to all, hunger will be a forgotten experience, the need for massive outside help will have passed, most nations will have entered a period of self-sustaining growth, and, although there will still be much to do, every American republic will be the master of its own revolution and its own hope and progress."

What President Kennedy proposed on that historic afternoon was a ten-year plan, "a plan to transform the 1960s into a decade of democratic progress."

Not since Bolívar's call for independence had a voice found such a resounding echo in Latin America. Five months later the Inter-American Economic and Social

Council had written the Charter of Punta del Este, which not only committed the American nations to the ideas and principles of the Alliance for Progress but had worked out in solid detail just what was needed, and would be aimed at, to make these principles work.

The Charter of Punta del Este sets a 2.5% increase in per capita income as its annual goal. At the same time it demands a more equitable distribution of national incomes, calling for agrarian reform where necessary to achieve this, and for a graduated income tax everywhere. The Charter urges basic change in risky national economies dependent on one or two crops, and suggests steps to encourage diversification in countries with such economies. It asks also for accelerated, rational industrialization, a steep and rapid increase in agricultural productivity, elimination of adult illiteracy, and the assurance that, by 1970, every child in the Americas will have access to at least six years of schooling.

The Charter of Punta del Este insists on a determined battle against infant mortality, to reduce the death rate of children under five by at least 50% before the decade is over. To this end, it sets the goal of providing adequate potable water and serviceable sewage to not less than 70% of the urban and 50% of the rural population.

The Charter demands as well a concerted attack on communicable diseases; improved nutrition; basic health services at both national and local levels; increased construction of low-cost housing; stable price levels; and cooperative arrangements to cure traditional wild fluctuations in the prices of the primary products of mine and soil, from the sale of which most of Latin America lives.

Finally, the Charter of Punta del Este looks toward "the strengthening of agreements on economic integration, with a view to the ultimate fulfillment of aspirations for a Latin American Common Market that will expand and diversify trade among the Latin American countries and thus contribute to the economic growth of the region."

An ambitious and generous program was mapped at Punta del Este, soundly based on the ambitious and generous convictions the Americas have shared from the moment of their independence.

In the preamble to the Charter of Punta del Este these convictions ring out:

"Almost two hundred years ago we began in this Hemisphere the long struggle for freedom which now inspires people in all parts of the world. Today, in ancient lands, men are moved to hope by the revolutions of our young nations' search for liberty.

"Now we give a new meaning to that revolutionary heritage. For America stands at a turning point in history. The men and women of our Hemisphere are reaching for the better life which today's skills have placed within their grasp. They are determined for themselves and their children to have decent and ever more abundant lives, to gain access to knowledge and equal opportunity for all, to end those conditions which benefit the few at the expense of the needs and dignity of the many.

"It is our inescapable task to fulfill these just desires— to demonstrate to the poor and forsaken of our countries, and of all lands, that the creative powers of free men hold the key to their progress and to the progress of future generations. And our certainty of ultimate success rests not alone on our faith in ourselves and in our nations but on the indomitable spirit of free man which has been the heritage of American civilization."

An idea so large, a plan so radical, was bound to encounter obstacles. In the United States, grumbling was heard that this Alliance for Progress was just another gigantic give-away, with Uncle Sam pouring his hard-earned resources down another alien rathole.

In Latin America, entrenched establishments were unwilling to let go of their privileges and prerogatives. There was suspicion as well that the *Alianza* was merely an attempt by the United States to buy allies in the cold war. Some Latin Americans clung to the even more distrustful notion that this whole Punta del Este project was simply the old U.S. intervention ploy under a fancy new guise.

As the program gathered momentum, however, many of the fears and reservations on both sides melted away. At Punta del Este the United States had pledged to put up to $20,000,000,000 into the Alliance effort, and the Latin American nations had undertaken to raise $80,000,000,000 from their own resources. (The gross national product of all Latin America was, at that time, less than one fifth of the goods and services produced in the United States.)

By mid-1965 the Latin American nations had invested more than $30,000,000,000 in their economic and social development and the United States pledge had been honored in about the same ratio. In addition, private investment moneys were beginning to flow into Latin America, both from the United States and from Western Europe. Japan, too, was showing interest.

More significant still, after a somewhat halting start in

New housing center under construction in Bogotá, Colombia;
(below) villager at work

1962, economic growth in Latin America had managed to meet the Alliance goal of 2.5% net increase per person in both 1963 and 1964. This was accomplished despite an exploding population which surged upward at a rate of 3% or more, requiring an economy expanding at a minimum rate of 5–6% a year to keep up with the target of the *Alianza*.

Also, by 1963, every country in Latin America had either drawn up or was working on a detailed, long-range development plan, and these plans were being checked by "nine wise men" whom the Latin American nations had chosen for the purpose.

In 1964 an Inter-American Committee on the Alliance for Progress was established, designed specifically to put the shoulders of all Latin American nations firmly to the *Alianza* wheel.

In 1965 the Latin American nations organized a Special Development Assistance Fund, to work on development projects requiring multinational solutions and multilateral agreements in and from Latin America.

That same year of 1965, the president of the Inter-American Committee, Dr. Carlos Sanz de Santamaria, noted that the time had passed when people in Latin America expected the Alliance to be a panacea conjuring electric plants out of the ground and producing a miraculous transformation of their continent.

"It is understood now," Dr. Sanz de Santamaria said, "that the Alliance is the decision of a group of free and sovereign nations to speed up their economic development and promote accelerated social progress, with or without external help, with or without technical assistance from abroad."

At the same time, with little more than one third of the Alliance decade completed, most of the reservations held in the United States had disappeared as well.

A Partners of the Alliance program had been developed in the U.S., under which states, cities, labor unions, civic clubs, business and professional groups, schools, co-operatives, universities, and even private individuals established direct contact with improvement or development groups in Latin America. By the end of 1964, twenty-five states in the U.S. had organized Partners of the Alliance Committees, and eighty-one U.S. towns had worked out sister-city relationships with Latin American counterparts.

Organized labor, working through the American Institute for Free Labor Development, had sponsored twenty-eight projects—low-cost housing, credit unions, workers' banks, consumer and producer co-operatives, medical clinics, rural development programs—planned by trade unions in thirteen *Alianza* nations.

The Pan American Development Foundation, a private organization created in 1964, had begun to channel south anything from a $1.20 contribution earned by an eight-year-old Texas schoolgirl to help Venezuelan first-graders, to a $28,000 donation of drugs from the Wyeth International Corporation for distribution in Central America.

Under this same program the Civinettes of Bethesda-Chevy Chase High School in Maryland put up a wishing well in a local shopping center to raise the funds that sent twenty desks and chairs to the Abraham Lincoln School in La Paz, Bolivia, and the Zale Jewelry Co. of Dallas, Texas, donated 1250 Braille watches to blind people in ten countries of Latin America.

With all its problems—and a rough row still to hoe—the

Alliance for Progress had taken root where it counted most, among the people of both continents.

In 1965, with two thirds of the development decade still to go, it was clear that there neither would be nor could be a turning back. The wheels of progress had been started, were moving and gathering momentum.

All wheels have small but vital hinges the absence of which can cause a breakdown. In economic development, statistics constitute these minuscule but indispensable components.

To make certain that progress would not be delayed by a lack of figures and facts, the Inter-American Statistical Institute, one of the oldest organizations in the system, was

The Alliance supplies funds for a new health clinic in Colombia

put into high gear as soon as Operation Pan America was proposed. The Statistical Institute persuaded and bullied, cajoled and sometimes nearly coerced the Latin American nations into forgoing their customary cavalier attitude toward figures, overcoming their embarrassment at what some of these figures revealed, and turning in accurate statistics based on up-to-date census taking.

Beginning in 1960, the Institute began to publish regularly a fat, dull, and extremely useful compendium called *America en Cifras* (*America in Figures*) which nose-counts everything from the occurrence of industrial disputes to the number of baths in urban and rural private dwelling units, from the state of a nation's balance of payments to its number of physicians, dentists, pharmacists, and veterinarians, and from an index of employment in mining and quarrying to the "cases of typhus, endemic, flea-borne, and epidemic, louse-borne."

In this age, all progress requires at some point a knowledge of the atom: how it works and what it can do for peace. To spread, develop, and co-ordinate such knowledge is the job of the Inter-American Nuclear Energy Commission (IANEC), created by the Council of the O.A.S. in April 1959.

The Commission, composed of one delegate from each American nation, meets at least once a year to review latest developments in the nuclear field and study their practical application to American needs.

At the Commission's meeting early in 1965, which took place at Puerto Rico's Nuclear Center, IANEC delegates had a particularly fascinating time. They were introduced

Students learn radioisotope techniques in international training course at Cornell University

to a nuclear reactor capable of producing electrical energy under conditions and on terms that make sense for the developing nations of Latin America.

The name of the reactor was "Bonus."

THE BANK
AND THE
BOARD

Imagine a bankers' board room dominated by a mysterious mask of glinting tin, matching stares with Don Quixote on the opposite wall; the mask, hand-fashioned by miners in Bolivia, surrounded by delicate Mayan pottery, haughty Aztec statues, and vivid Inca cloth; and the collection facing an enormous map of the Americas, with blue and red bands streaming from a central core like refracted rays of a summer sun.

The core is marked "Washington," which is headquarters for the Inter-American Development Bank. The red and blue streamers, reaching into the most remote corners of Central and South America, are loans made by that bank since it began operations early in 1960.

If the board room is extraordinary, so is the bank itself. It upsets almost every cliché coined about banks and and bankers.

The cliché says banks are conservative: the Inter-American Development Bank is a major advocate of social and economic change in the Americas.

The Inter-American Development Bank

The stereotype has it that banks will not lend you money unless you can prove fairly convincingly that you do not really need it, or at least can afford to do without it. In financial parlance, this requirement is known as security or, more specifically, collateral.

The Inter-American Development Bank specializes in lending money to enterprises, public or private, which cannot raise funds anywhere else, because the undertaking is primarily a response to need and was funded in the first place by hope.

Banks are interested in cold cash, says the adage, not human requirements or resources. The Inter-American Development Bank lends money to bring clean drinking water to the crowded, poverty-stricken inhabitants of

Latin America's slums. It provides financing for the tools, the seed, the machinery, the credit needed by formerly landless peasants now settled on their own pieces of ground. It helps to maintain many of the volatile, articulate universities in Latin America whose students are among the most demonstrative proponents of progress, demanding as a minimum immediate and rapid change and as a maximum violent revolution.

In a culminating reversal of generally held beliefs about financial institutions, the Inter-American Development Bank considers all these unorthodox undertakings important achievements.

BID, as it is known throughout Latin America (_Banco Interamericano de Desarrollo_), is another of those historic hemisphere dreams which slowly evolved into waking determination and finally hardened into fact.

In the case of the bank, the process began in 1890 at the first Inter-American Conference. Latin delegates to that Washington meeting discussed the desirability of having an inter-American financial institution. The United States vaguely concurred but no one did anything. The U.S. was not ready to involve itself in so concrete a manner, and the Latin American nations also shied away from a project requiring so firm a multinational commitment.

Everyone agreed that an inter-American Bank would be a good idea but, like Sleeping Beauty, it lay attractively dormant for practically fairy-tale time. In more realistic reckoning, it was for almost seventy years.

Prince Charming arrived at last in the rather incongruous shape of IA-ECOSOC, the Inter-American Economic and

Social Council. IA-ECOSOC had been instructed by an Economic Conference of the Organization of American States, meeting in Buenos Aires in August and September of 1957, "to seek formulas that would permit the expansion of the economic development of Latin America, especially through proposals for establishment of an Inter-American Bank for economic development."

IA-ECOSOC went to work on the assignment, and suddenly all the reluctance which had paralyzed action in this area for close to three quarters of a century disappeared. In August 1958 the United States officially told IA-ECOSOC that it was in favor of establishing such a bank and willing to participate in it. Within weeks every one of the Latin-American nations had expressed the same sentiment, pledged the same commitment.

By September 1958 the Foreign Ministers of twenty-one American republics (Cuba was then still an active member of the O.A.S.) had agreed that the bank should be founded —right then. IA-ECOSOC was instructed to work out details and draft the required agreement. The agreement was to go into effect as soon as countries representing 85% of the bank's capital subscription had signed and ratified it.

This was accomplished by December 30, 1959, and two months later the Inter-American Development Bank was in business, with 60% of its capital subscribed by Latin America, a Chilean president, and seven directors, six of whom were Latin Americans. The structure is still the same. Two thirds of the bank's staff is Latin American as well, and the bank's primary working language is Spanish.

To the surprise of many on both American continents, the bank was a phenomenal success from the start. Upsetting two additional long-honored clichés—that banks are invariably cautious, and Latin Americans incurably addicted to the concept of *mañana,* the policy of let-us-not-do-today-what-can-be-done-tomorrow—the Inter-American Development Bank had, by the end of 1961, allocated $282,000,000 in loans for industry, housing, hospitals, health, schools, agriculture, mines, livestock, forest exploitation, and national and regional development agencies.

At the end of three years it had tripled its ordinary capital resources to exceed $2,000,000,000; had sold six bond issues—in the U.S., Italy, the Federal Republic of Germany, and the United Kingdom—totaling $272,600,-000; and was getting offers of participation capital from private sources, investment groups, and banks, from Pennsylvania to Puerto Rico.

When in April 1965 the Inter-American Development Bank loaned $7,000,000 to a financial institution in Peru to expand a credit program for small and medium-sized industries, eleven commercial banks participated in the loan, without BID's guarantee.

The record the Inter-American Development Bank had established in three years of operation was such that not only were private citizens in the U.S. and Europe ready to stake their own money on it, but also hard-nosed U.S. banks were prepared to take on faith its financial judgment —in the traditionally risky area of Latin America.

The bank is housed in a very plain, very functional building in the center of Washington and has, of course, no public floor with tellers in their cages. But bank president Felipe Herrera likes to think of the bank as having three windows, handling the three different types of loans the bank makes.

The First Window deals with "hard," purely commercial loans, carrying an interest rate of between 5% and 6%, and repayable in the currency in which the loan is made. Half of the money lent from Window No. 1 has gone to private enterprise to provide financing for such undertakings as a fishing and port facility in Chile, the manufacture of automotive parts in Argentina and Brazil, the erection of cement factories in Peru and in Costa Rica, irrigation projects in Chile and in Mexico, development of the sheep industry in Ecuador, textile plants in Guatemala, corn flour mills in Honduras and Nicaragua, and a bread and *tortilla* factory in El Salvador.

The Second Window deals with special loans. The bank has a separate Fund for Special Operations which is administered quite independently from its ordinary capital. This fund does precisely what its name implies: it provides the financing for special projects which make sound development sense but for which commercial capital cannot be raised, or could be raised only on terms too disadvantageous for the borrower to afford. Loans made from Window No. 2 are usually long-term, at low interest rates, with high amortization allowances, and repayments not necessarily in dollars or hard currency but in the currency of the borrowing nation.

Characteristic examples of Window No. 2 loans are the $4,800,000 lent to the Bolivian Mining Corporation, an autonomous public institution, to overhaul its operations and enable it to become a profit-making enterprise again. Or the $1,000,000 lent to Costa Rica to encourage and develop co-operatives of small farmers and fishermen. Window No. 2 also pays for necessary research and pre-investment studies and, sometimes, for the experts who do

*The Bank helps finance low-income housing in Chile (above)
and a water sewerage plant in Venezuela (below)*

the research or advise a government, a bank, or even private industry in the technical facts about a projected undertaking.

The bank's Third Window administers the Social Progress Trust Fund, another financial instrument for development purposes, which the United States Government capitalized as one of its contributions to the Alliance for Progress. The Social Progress Trust Fund operates with about $500,000,000, with the moneys earmarked entirely for social development projects in four basic areas: land settlement and improved land use; housing for low-income groups; community water supply and sanitary facilities; and advanced education and training.

From Window No. 3 had come, at the end of the first eighteen months of the fund's existence, housing for 270,000 people; 123 water and sewage systems benefiting 300 communities with a population of just under 3,000,000; and new leases on a productive life for 100,000 landless or low-income farmers.

Part of the success and the popularity of the Inter-American Development Bank is due to the bank's alertness to every aspect of development needs, including human ones. Another part is due to its extraordinary flexibility. The bank, after having disbursed more than $500,000,000, does not have a formal printed loan application, and has no intention of getting one. The directors consider every request on its own full merit and they know that live needs cannot be frozen into dead formulas. The bank encourages would-be borrowers to sit down and spell out their requirements as they see them, either in writing or in person, coming into the bank or talking to the bank's regional representatives. This has to be done by the principals involved. BID does not deal with middlemen.

While the bank tries to offer an immediate response to borrowers' needs, it takes a long view of its responsibilities.

It is convinced, for example, that the most fundamental development resource of all is the human resource, particularly the scientific, technical, economic, and political leaders of the future. A bank study shows that Latin America today has one quarter of one technician for every thousand persons in the population, compared to seven per thousand in the United States. Productivity and prosperity follow a predictable parallel.

The bank, therefore, has made participation in the stepping up of higher education in Latin America one of its basic concerns. With BID money, lent either to governments for programs of higher education or directly to universities, full-fledged institutions of advanced training have increased from 160 in 1961, with a total of 520,000 students, to 196 in 1966, with a total of 680,000 students. The bank expects to "graduate" 1,000,000 students a year by 1970.

Another far-reaching project for which the bank considers itself intimately responsible is the economic integration of Latin America. Already the bank has lent money from its special fund to launch regional industries and infra-structure projects in the Central American Common Market. It has financed the export of manufactured goods from one member of LAFTA, the still floundering Latin American Free Trade Association, to another. BID president Herrera, today one of the most influential men in the hemisphere, is an outspoken and tireless advocate of the early and complete integration of Latin America, both economically and politically.

United in spirit and power, the president of the Inter-American Development Bank points out, Latin America rose to claim its political independence. United the same way, it can achieve its economic freedom. The bank, he holds, could be the Bolívar of that battle.

There exists yet another organization deeply involved in an imaginative push toward progress in Latin America. As unusual as the bank in its approaches and policies, the Inter-American Defense Board, military high command of the hemisphere, is entrusted with the mission of co-ordinating common defense measures and creating the broadest possible basis for military co-operation in the Americas.

Frequently referred to as the "Inter-American Chiefs of Staff," the Board is tucked away in a pink gingerbread house in Washington's silent and sumptuous diplomatic section. There it maps strategy and tactics designed to keep the hemisphere secure from both external and internal aggression.

The Inter-American Defense Board precedes the O.A.S. as an instrument of the inter-American system. It was established one month after the Japanese attack on Pearl Harbor, which made the Americas realize that no one was safe from Axis aggression. Meeting in Rio de Janeiro in January 1942, the Foreign Ministers of the twenty-one American republics ordered "the immediate meeting in Washington of a commission composed of military and naval technicians appointed by each of the Governments

*Major General Samaniego, minister from Paraguay, presides
at meeting of Inter-American Defense Board, July 1959*

to study and recommend to them the measures necessary
for the defense of the American Continents."

In March these defense experts met in the Hall of the
Americas—one occasion on which that beautiful room
served a grim purpose—and devised the plans which successfully scotched all attempts by the Axis powers to gain a
foothold anywhere in the American hemisphere.

During World War II the Inter-American Defense Board
worked out ways to eliminate clandestine telecommunica-
tion stations; designed plane-spotting methods; devised
anti-sabotage security; and planned the co-ordination and
safeguarding of strategic materials. The Board also mapped
the establishment and location of naval and air bases; anti-

submarine defense; standardization of military materials, training, and organization; and the teaching of the American continents' languages in military schools to eliminate, at least on the command level, the language barrier between the defenders of the hemisphere.

With these measures as a foundation, the Americas succeeded in World War II in turning back all Axis attempts at infiltrating the hemisphere; hermetically closed the Panama Canal to enemy traffic; kept the Gulf of Mexico and the tight passages of the Caribbean safely open to Allied shipping, and arranged for Latin America to supply many of the strategic materials which were needed for the Allied war effort.

When Germany tried, in South America, to have some of her war vessels crash the continental security barriers, the ships were chased back to sea, where the British Navy caught and demolished them. In addition, Brazil sent land and air forces to fight in Europe.

By 1948, when the Charter of the O.A.S. was written, the Board had proven its value so clearly that it was converted into a permanent organ of the inter-American system. Its "commander" was to be the newly established O.A.S. Advisory Defense Committee, composed of the highest military authorities of the American states.

The Board's budget is met by the Pan American Union.

Like all other inter-American bodies, the Inter-American Defense Board has no weighted voting. Every country has an equal vote and while the Board's chairman is a general officer of the country in which the Board functions—i.e., the United States—the vice-chairmanship is allocated by lot, on a non-repeat rotation basis. Board protocol calls for the seating of delegates in alphabetical order of the countries they represent.

Settling down to its task within the O.A.S. framework, the Board continued its detailed preparations for collective defense: from composing a dictionary of military terms to ascertain that a military command means exactly the same in every American country, to the standardization of maps and charts, of ground signals for air traffic control, of aviation fuels and lubricants.

One member of the Inter-American Defense Board, tapping his pencil on a thick sheaf of studies, said: "These things may not sound very important to civilians in peacetime, but you take that last item, for example, fuels and lubricants. If a military plane landed for refueling and they didn't have the right kind to service it, the plane would be useless, out of commission for practical purposes. In war, that kind of thing can make the difference between victory and defeat."

Taking a step more self-evident to the civilian mind, the Board established an Inter-American Defense College at Fort McNair, at which military officers of all the American nations, and from the three branches of the armed services, are given advanced training.

Two years after the Inter-American Defense Board had been put under the O.A.S. roof a new challenge emerged in the hemisphere which clearly came under the Board's jurisdiction. By 1951 it had become evident that aggression in the Americas would henceforth have a new facet, an internal aspect for which new measures and methods of defense were needed.

In April 1951, America's Foreign Ministers decided that

"the expansionist activities of international Communism require the immediate adoption of measures to safeguard the peace and the security of the continent."

Eleven years later Soviet missiles in Cuba proved how accurate that estimate had been. The missiles put within their deadly range not only the southern part of the United States but all of Mexico, Colombia, Venezuela, Ecuador, northern Brazil, the six countries of Central America and, of course, the other islands of the Caribbean.

In the intervening years the Inter-American Defense Board, in addition to planning protection against overt attack, had also devised a tactic to battle the new kind of aggression, a tactic designed to reach as deep and take as long a view as do the Communists in their strategy of subversion.

The Board had decided that the armed forces of Latin America should attempt to combat this subtle subversion with constructive projects. When not engaged in military training, the armed forces were put to work in a program known as *Acción Cívica Militar* (Military Civic Action). This program sends soldiers into the backlands to help build roads and bridges, schools and health centers. It uses the air force to fly the sick in jungle outposts or on remote islands and inaccessible villages to the nearest air force base for medical treatment. It has navies transport X-ray equipment, doctors, nurses, medical supplies, and drinking water to settlements which have seen little or nothing of such modern contributions to health.

Under the *Acción Cívica Militar* program army trucks now carry powdered milk or high-protein mush to schools, to give hundreds of thousands of children in Latin America

the only nutritionally sound meal of their day. Army engineers are breaking through tangled jungle terrain to build roads, and they make Christmas toys for orphans in their spare time. Army veterinarians inseminate cattle for farmers, and army technicians drill wells for villages.

At the same time the armed forces throughout Latin America launched a program to give vocational as well as military training to recruits, particularly Indian recruits, who will go back to their farms and hamlets and there put to use their newly acquired skills. Perhaps most important of all, the armed forces of Latin America now teach their illiterate recruits to read and write and, in some countries, print books and organize classes for civilian adults who never had the chance to go to school.

The idea behind *Acción Cívica Militar* is to convince the peoples of today's Latin America that, whatever may have been the role of the military in the past, or the lot and behavior of soldiers, the armed forces of today are on the people's side, concerned not only with their security and protection but with their progress and welfare in every way.

The strategy seems to be sound. Wherever *Acción Cívica Militar* has penetrated and done an effective job, Communist guerrillas are having difficulty getting a foothold.

With all its traditional and novel ramifications, perhaps the most interesting aspects of the Inter-American Defense Board are its limitations. One of these is illustrated startlingly at Board headquarters in Washington. Because Cuba has not been expelled from the Organization of American States, only suspended as long as its government pursues aggressive and interventionist policies, and because the Cuban people are still considered members of the inter-American family and an integral component of the inter-American system, the Board flies the flag of Cuba along with those of the other twenty American republics on all ceremonial occasions. In the Board's staff room, and on its table of organization, a place is designated and kept open for the Republic of Cuba. The hope and trust is that these spaces will not be empty forever, or even for very long.

The other limitation under which the Board operates is even more meaningful. The same resolution which established the Inter-American Defense Board as an organ of the O.A.S. also says that whenever the American nations decide, by a two-thirds majority, to consider the Board's labor ended, it shall cease to function.

The resolution demonstrates that Bolívar's conviction, that war is not a proper tool for free and independent nations to use in their conduct with each other, persists in the thinking of the Americas.

THE BIG
PARTNERS

When one looks at the complex apparatus needed to govern men in this age, it is not always easy to recognize that the basic ingredients of political institutions are people, and the fundamental components of an international organization the individual nations that belong to it. They give it life, color, and meaning. They create its problems and solve them.

The Organization of American States is no exception to this rule. While the O.A.S. incorporates a shared dream and reflects the glow of hope for a finer future, it is also a composite of the historical, political, and cultural make-up of the different nations under its roof; a place where the personalities of the member states encounter each other, sometimes merge, and occasionally clash.

These personalities vary widely, giving to the O.A.S. its excitement, its brilliance and its stimulus, while creating also its difficulties, its misunderstandings, and in some situations its cross-purposes.

96

The O.A.S. has three big partners—aside from the United States, which is the giant of the system. They are Argentina, Brazil, and Mexico. Together these three range over almost the entire hemisphere south of the U.S.A. and cover more than 5,000,000 square miles.

There are great differences between them in geography, climate, and resources and, as a consequence, in history, culture, and in their attitudes toward the Organization of American States.

Argentina, a mammoth 1,072,700-square-mile triangle reaching from the southernmost tip of the continent up to the Tropic of Capricorn, has a tradition of cordial coolness toward the hemispheric family.

Argentina's José de San Martín campaigned with Bolívar for the liberation of South America from Spain and tried, as did Bolívar, to prevent the continental fragmentation that followed. But they failed in their time and Argentina, having fought free, turned its attention inward, to its enormous pampas, tempting and forbidding at the same time. These great plains, where the knee-high grass waved endlessly like the sea, produced the *gauchos,* Argentina's cowboys, a race of fearless, lawless men who with their bravery and recklessness, their ingenuity and endurance, conquered the plains to raise the cattle and grow the wheat that laid the foundations for Argentina's wealth.

The Argentine economy has changed since the *gauchos* built its base in the first half of the last century. Argentina today is one of the most industrialized of the Latin American nations and is striving for a development in which agriculture and industry will balance each other, to make

A group of gauchos, the colorful cowboys of the Argentinian plains

for more even and more secure growth. But the people of the Argentine still eat better than anyone else in Latin America and their output per person, as well as their income and consumption per person, is among the highest in the southern half of the hemisphere.

This was not achieved easily. The *gauchos* and their ways and attitudes created prosperity but brought to their country also a climate of political instability, a reliance on power rather than law, a penchant for violence instead of an instinct for compromise.

When, in the course of the past century and a half, Argentina was not preoccupied with her own economic or political problems, she tended to look east, to Europe, from her 1600-mile coastline on the Atlantic Ocean.

Argentina's main trading partner has traditionally been Europe, and still is today. Ninety-five per cent of her population is of European descent, of Spanish, Italian, English, German, and Slavic strains. Of all the nations of Latin America, Argentina kept her doors open widest to continued immigration from Europe after she won her independence. European ties, European loyalties, European hankerings are strong still in the Argentine and play an important role in the nation's political orientation.

During World War II the influence of Argentinians of German and Italian descent prevented the nation from becoming involved on the Allied side until the war was almost over. Not until 1945 did Argentina finally throw

54111

Chipboard plant in Argentina

in her lot with the other countries of the Americas by declaring war on the Axis.

After the war Argentina did participate in all Pan American efforts to organize hemispheric solidarity and bring peace and progress through combined effort; but her attitude and her relationship to the inter-American system were still remote, detached, and as noncommittal as enlightened self-interest and international good manners allowed.

Lately—very lately—that attitude has begun to change. Argentine sentiment toward her American neighbors is warming as the nation discovers that having friends in your own back yard is a comfortable feeling.

When the former Argentine dictator Juan Domingo Perón tried, late in 1964, to stage a comeback to the nation he had misruled for a decade, bankrupting it in the process, Brazil foiled the attempt. Not only did Brazil refuse to let Perón proceed to Argentina when his plane landed on Brazilian territory, she also turned down his request to base himself and his political maneuvers in Brazil. She insisted that the plane which had brought Perón take off again immediately for its point of origin, Spain. Brazilians did not just want Perón out of Argentina's way. For safety's sake, they wanted him out of America's way.

Having witnessed what one good neighbor on the continent can do to forestall trouble, and what the Organization of American States did when it severed relations with Cuba to curb mischief made from the opposite political corner, Argentina's physician President Arturo U. Illia became a staunch convert to the inter-American system. The Organization of American States, he advocated in

1965, should be strengthened, and activated politically to a point where it would be capable of preventing "minority leaders" of any political persuasion from plotting the destruction of freely constituted governments.

Economically, too, Argentina has begun to discover that inter-American efforts can pay dividends. Argentina has joined the Latin American Free Trade Association and, slowly but inevitably, is developing trade ties within the Americas.

Still, the nation, and important persons in the nation, are of two minds in their attitude toward the inter-American system. The smile with which Argentina regards the idea of Pan American Union and the institution of the O.A.S. is a Mona Lisa smile. No one is ever quite sure what it means, including, one suspects, the lady who does the smiling.

On Pan American Day, April 14, 1965, Dr. Ricardo Miguel Colombo, ambassador extraordinary and plenipotentiary of Argentina to the Organization of American States, turned over the ground in the garden of the House of the Americas with a golden spade, planted a tree symbolic of Argentina's devotion to the soil of the hemisphere, and paid eloquent tribute to the Pan American idea. Not only, said he,. would this idea make of the Americas a hemisphere in which peace is guaranteed, but it presented also a dynamic protagonist of a multinational effort for democratic development and the development of democracy.

Ambassador Colombo received a warm round of applause when he finished, and many *abrazos* in the garden of the House of the Americas.

But a day later, discussing the O.A.S. in the privacy of his own embassy, his concern was largely with the favorite hobby horses of non-commitment: self-determination and non-intervention. He conceded that political peace, social tranquillity, and economic development would all be substantially aided by a smoothly working inter-American system, and had progressed quite some way under the aegis of the O.A.S. "But," he insisted, "I strongly believe, for example, that Cuba should be left to solve her own problems. I would not want to intefere with her in any way, just as I would not want her to interfere with us."

The fact that an O.A.S. mission had found in Venezuela concrete evidence of active armed Cuban interference, or even the fact that Cuba had asked for, and received, atomic missiles from the Soviet Union aimed at her American neighbors, somehow had not managed to pierce the traditional Argentinian detachment. An Argentine general, who came to call on the ambassador and heard the remarks about Cuba, quietly pointed out that Havana had by her own admission trained 10,000 Latin American "revolutionary experts" within three years. The ambassador nodded slowly but added nothing to the statement he had made.

Two weeks later Dr. Colombo was in strife-torn Santo Domingo as chairman of the O.A.S. Special Committee trying to restore peace in the Dominican Republic. The Committee he led recommended the immediate formation of an Inter-American Peace Force. It suggested that the O.A.S. request governments of member states "to make contingents of their land, naval, air or police forces available immediately . . . to form an inter-American force."

Argentina was not among the nations that responded to the urgent call of Ambassador Colombo's committee. The Argentinian President was in favor, as was the Minister of Defense. But in the spring of 1965 the Argentine Congress still said no.

The first Latin American nation to respond to the call was Brazil. It also sent the largest Latin American contingent. A Brazilian general was named to command the first Inter-American Peace Force in action.

No one demurred and no one was surprised. Brazil, enormous (just about the size of the U.S.), secure in its multiracial homogeneity, and rich in resources as yet untapped, is and consistently has been one of the most solid supporters of the inter-American system. The Organization of American States has always found Brazil dependable in both word and deed.

In many ways Brazil has had an easier time in the New World than its Hispanic neighbors. Portuguese by derivation, it was discovered in 1500 by the Portuguese navigator Pedro Alvares Cabral, who claimed it for his sovereign King Manuel I.

The fifteenth and sixteenth centuries were glorious times for Portugal. Even earlier than Spain, Portugal had sent its explorers to sail to fabled lands through uncharted seas. It was a Portuguese, Vasco da Gama, who first reached India by sea, sailing around Africa and the Cape of Good Hope. Da Gama himself helped organize the expedition of Cabral and instructed his navigator compatriot.

Just what took Cabral so far off his intended course—he too was originally headed for India around Africa's southern tip—is not certain. Whether the exploration was intentional or he was driven there by storms, Cabral reached the continent of South America. He named the land he saw Vera Cruz, and thought it a land tongue of Asia.

None of the famous navigators of the time, Portuguese or Spanish, really believed that they had discovered a new continent. All hoped they had found a passage to China. They were convinced that the Antilles, the Caribbean island chain which includes Cuba, Haiti, and the Dominican Republic, Trinidad, Tobago, and Jamaica, were Asian offshore islands.

The first to realize that this new-found land was neither India nor China was Amerigo Vespucci, a Florentine who sailed for both Spain and Portugal. Vespucci's first voyage brought him to South America in 1499. He was back in 1501, explored for a year along the northeastern coast, charted and calculated, and came up with his historic conclusion: that this was a continent no one in Europe had ever heard of. It was 1507 before Vespucci was believed. Then the new continent was named in his honor: America.

Cabral's "Vera Cruz" was the beginning of a Portuguese realm in this New World. Almost as soon as it had been ascertained that indeed a whole new world had been discovered, the monarchs of Spain and Portugal, devout Catholics both, asked the Pope to divide the new continent between them. The papal division resulted in the carving of a giant triangle in the heart of that even larger triangle that is South America, the former allocated to Portugal, the latter to Spain. In terms of territory, the division was about even. But the Portuguese realm had the advantage of being

one solid mass, while the Spanish territories surrounded it
—north, south, and west, like a massive necklace around a
very full throat.

Perhaps it was being surrounded in this way that made
the Portuguese possession so cohesive from the start. Perhaps, too, it was the different nature of the Portuguese
monarchy, softer and more flexible than the Spanish, producing overseas a society which had a looser weave, could
and did encompass white strands and red, black, and
yellow.

Brazil never had to fight for her independence. Characteristically, the country's name had been changed from
Vera Cruz by early settlers who found a dyewood named
pau-brasil which turned out to be a very lucrative export.
It was the staff of their lives and they gratefully named their
country after it. There were no objections from Lisbon.

There were no objections from Lisbon either when Brazil declared her independence on September 27, 1822. In
fact it was Dom Pedro, son of Portugal's King João VI, who
read the declaration of independence and was proclaimed
Brazil's emperor. Dom Pedro's son, Pedro II, poet, scholar,
scientist, was popular, deeply concerned with his people,
and proud of being an American. Largely because of the
tone he set, Brazil did not become a republic until 1889,
the last American nation to emerge from the monarchial
cocoon. When Latin America sent its representatives to
Washington for the first Inter-American Conference in
1889 the Brazilian delegate represented his emperor. The
change from empire to federal republic, which took place
in November of that year, was accomplished without vio-

lence or bloodshed. And the Brazilian delegate's orders from home never changed. Both empire and republic were interested in an inter-American system.

Brazil has had—and still has—its problems. They are economic, and because the country is so enormous the problems are enormous also.

Although Rio de Janeiro, major port and former capital of Brazil, is a scintillating metropolis, hunger has stalked the northeast of the country for centuries. São Paulo, hard-driving entrepreneur city of the nation, resembles Manhattan in its downtown section, with skyscrapers reaching for the clouds, but vast tracts of land along the Amazon River are still unused and largely unexplored. Brasilia, the nation's new capital, is probably the most imaginative city created by twentieth-century man, with its grace of curved concrete, glass, steel, sculpture, and brilliant mosaic, offering the refreshing wonder of an oasis in the desert center of the land, but Brazil still has enormous iron mines it has not touched, powerful waterfalls untapped for electricity, an array of minerals lying idle in the ground, and vast forest resources that just rot away.

Brazil's almost 80,000,000 people still produce less, and therefore earn less on the average, than do the people of most other nations on the South American continent.

The country is aware of this lag and prepared to face up to it. She is one of the most energetic advocates of the Latin American Free Trade Association and, within the American family, one of the most outspoken critics of everyone, including herself.

Her ambassador to the Organization of American States has chastised Latin America—emphatically including Bra-

A graceful modern structure in Brasilia, the new capital of Brazil

zil—for being proud and unrealistic, and has flayed the United States for being self-centered in its political attitudes and provincial in its trade practices.

"But," adds Brazil's O.A.S. Ambassador Ilmar Penna Marinho, "we are all learning. In Latin America we now recognize that we are underdeveloped and that we can and must change. There is a new realism and a new sense of proportion.

"And in the United States, I see a new, and much-needed, concern with the hemisphere."

As for the Organization of American States, Brazil believes that the inter-American system needs strengthening.

Unlike some of the more formal-minded of the Latin American nations, Brazil is of the opinion that the Charter of the O.A.S. is fine as written but needs more energetic and sustained enforcement. It may require updating in one or two points, Brazil holds, and certainly the structure built on the O.A.S. Charter and branching out from it can stand streamlining.

The system should also, in Ambassador Penna Marinho's descriptive word, be "dynamized." Brazil would like to see a Pan American summit meeting once a year by having the Inter-American Conferences put on a regular annual basis. Brazil also wants the Inter-American Peace Committee upgraded into a full-fledged Council and given the same kind of muscle that the Economic and Social Council has acquired over the past decade.

It is Brazil's belief that, in today's world, the United Nations cannot do very much for the Americas. The U.N., Brazil notes, is torn by the deep and demanding ideological schism of the cold war, and cleft in a different way by the struggle within the organization between the have and have-not nations, with the latter increasingly powerful in voice and vote and the former increasingly unwilling to submit to policies not of their making.

To Brazil, the role played by the United Nations in the Dominican Republic flare-up in 1965 is a glaring demonstration of why the Americas are best advised to set their house in order by themselves. As Brazil sees it, to the United Nations the crisis in the Dominican Republic was troubled water in which some of its members could fish. The Soviet Union immediately attempted to turn the conflict into a cold war issue, coupling it, in its propaganda at the United Nations and throughout the world, with the war in Viet Nam. France, launched on its Gaullist policy of opposing the United States as a matter of principle, hoping thereby to bolster her own Europe-centered interests, took advantage of the platform offered by the United Nations Security Council to use Santo Domingo as a convenient stick with which to beat the U.S.

Even U.N. Secretary-General U Thant's personal team in the Dominican Republic seemed to be as interested in pointing up differences as in finding solutions.

"On balance," Ambassador Penna Marinho summed up after the Dominican experience, "I believe that the O.A.S. is the only tool which can solve our American problems. Besides, it is the best system yet devised of collective co-operation. For our own sake, and as an example to the rest of the world, we should keep it, strengthen it, and make it work in every area of our lives. Brazil believes this can be done."

The third of the big partners in the Inter-American system, Mexico, behaves in the American family somewhat as France behaves in the West European family.

Articulately committed to the Pan American idea from the beginning, an energetic leader in the early days of organization of the system (the second Inter-American Conference in 1901–2 was held in Mexico), it is now as a rule a negative force in the Organization of American States, verging occasionally on the destructive.

Mexico is the only member of the O.A.S. which still ignores the Organization's decision to sever diplomatic and economic ties with the Castro government. This despite the

Inter-American Peace Conference was held in Mexico in 1945

fact that the Soviet atomic missiles imported by Castro had all of Mexico within range.

Mexico also opposed formation and use of the Inter-American Peace Force in the Dominican Republic and objected strongly to having an Inter-American Peace Force put on a permanent stand-by basis. When the idea was broached, Mexico threatened to take the issue to the International Court of Justice at The Hague, thus undermining the Inter-American Peace Force in two ways: first, by attempting to have it declared illegal and, second, by taking an American issue out of the inter-American system when everyone else in that system believes it can and should be settled within the hemisphere.

When Mexico's ambassador to the Organization of American States, suave and sage Don Rafael de la Colina, speaks of his country's fears of "superstructures" and objections to "superstates," he sounds like the voice of General de Gaulle transcribed for America.

There are reasons for Mexico's extreme sensitivity on the subject of untrammeled sovereignty—historical reasons which still cast long and somber shadows.

At a time when the other nations of the Americas were struggling, however haphazardly, toward unity, cohesion, stability, Mexico was literally torn apart. And torn apart from the outside. The war with the United States (1846–48) cost Mexico almost two fifths of her territory, the lands that are now Texas, California, New Mexico, and parts of Arizona.

Sixteen years later the long hand of Europe reached across the ocean from the France of Napoleon III, and the overlord of France succeeded in 1864 in foisting on Mexico a European emperor, Archduke Maximilian of Austria.

While this anachronistic attempt at Old World meddling with the New World wound up in predictable failure— well-meaning but hopelessly unpopular Maximilian was assassinated, his wife Charlotte went mad, and the French court abandoned its overseas adventure as nonchalantly as it had been launched—the scars left on Mexico were deep.

Mexico still remembers that, when the United States wrested from it its northern territories, the nations of Latin America were unhappy but did nothing. And when Na-

poleon put his Austrian protégé on a throne thrust at re-
publican Mexico by imperial France, no one came to help,
or even offered to, from either one of the Americas.

Through these two national tragedies, inflicted on her
from within and without the hemisphere, Mexico learned
the bitter lesson of standing alone. She has not forgotten it.

Adding to her tendency to depend on no one is the effective job she has done on the economic front, pulling herself
up by the proverbial bootstraps. The Mexican economic
achievement is all the more impressive because, when it
was begun, the poverty of the country was such that an
overwhelming proportion of its population had neither
boot nor shoe nor even sandal.

A revolution in 1910 resulted in a united nation setting
itself political, social, and economic goals which were never
lost sight of again. In the half century that followed,
Mexico promulgated an extensive agrarian reform, dou-
bled its literacy, and laid the foundations for a modern
economy. Since World War II, industry in Mexico has
taken giant strides, giving the industrial center of Monter-
rey the well-earned nickname of "Pittsburgh south of the
border."

Mexico's almost 40,000,000 people have had a sustained
and heady taste of both political stability and economic
progress which they feel they owe to no one but themselves.

Mexico's big bugaboo is intervention, her major concern
self-determination. She insists that the Organization of
American States must be an association of equals, and
though willing to concede that it indeed is that in both
principle and law, she feels that it is up to the weaker states

in the Organization to be, as Ambassador de la Colina put it, "particularly jealous of the principle."

Oddly, Mexico, though second in population and third in area among the Latin American nations, persists in regarding herself as one of the weak members of the O.A.S. whose business it is to be jealous of their rights.

Ambassador de la Colina explains this attitude by pointing out that in the modern world it is not physical size or the number of inhabitants that count in essaying a nation's strength. It is, he says, "a matter of industrialization and self-containment."

The Mexican ambassador never mentions military strength. He admits that today's Mexico has nothing to fear from the military giant of the hemisphere, the United States. He concedes in addition that the United States is honestly pledged to the principle of equality in the Americas and exercises no pressure, through either power or wealth, on Mexico.

"But," he comments sadly, "there is a history of pressures and of wars."

Mexico's ambassador to the O.A.S. takes a very long view of history. He looks back at the social development of man and sees five thousand years of violence as the approved method of settling differences, and only about four hundred years of attempts to find solutions through law.

It does not disturb him then to see the inter-American system grow slowly, in very careful stages, heading for an equilibrium he envisages in the future in which the economy of the United States will be integrated with that of Latin America and there will be no more cause for anyone in the hemisphere to be jealous of principles which guarantee equality.

In the meantime, even Ambassador de la Colina holds that "we Americans have done better than anyone else in the world in achieving equality, and the Organization of American States is improving every day."

As he makes the statement, a philosophical smile flits across his face.

"In time," he adds, "everything is perfectible."

IN THE
MIDDLE

Eight nations in Latin America belong to a middle group in the American family. They find themselves in the middle in a number of ways: in size, in population, in power, as well as in their relationships with North America, Latin America, and the Organization of American States.

There is considerable diversity within the middle group. Its members range from Colombia, with its almost 500,000 square miles of territory, 15,000,000 people, and pride in high culture, to Paraguay, with only 157,000 square miles, less than 2,000,000 inhabitants, and a history of warfare, valor, and long-lasting dictatorships.

The middle group includes Peru, which also extends over about 500,000 square miles and contains a population of 11,000,000, deeply absorbed in the fascinating past of both Indian Inca and Spanish classic traditions but beginning now to grow explosively into modernity. And Uruguay, a small oblong of a land with 72,172 square miles, 3,000,000 people, a future-minded, homogeneous population of Spanish and Italian descent, progressive, democratic—and in economic trouble because of its concentration on only two major products, livestock and wool.

Ecuador, too, tropical, colorful, proud to be the producer of what the world calls "Panama hats," belongs to the middle eight, with an area of 116,270 square miles hugging the equator from the Pacific to the Andes, and a population of 5,000,000, a large portion of it pure Indian. So does oil-rich Venezuela, whose 8,000,000 persons, living in 352,000 square miles, have the highest per capita income of the entire Latin American continent and, within recent years, forward-looking democratic governments, determined to make the benefits of Venezuela's black gold flow to all segments of the population. And Bolivia, potentially wealthy owner of 416,000 square miles of land rich in minerals—tin, copper, lead, zinc, antimony, bismuth, wolfram, gold, tungsten, petroleum—but corroded still by poverty which afflicts major segments of its 4,000,000 population.

Finally, the middle group comprises Chile, with 286,000 square miles of territory stretching along the Pacific coast in a slim but extended sliver reaching more than halfway down the Latin American continent, from the subtropical latitude of 20° to the freezing Tierra del Fuego at 55° south.

Chile's 8,000,000 population is a mixture of Spanish and Araucanian Indian, one of the few Indian groups who were never defeated by force of arms. Chile also has a sprinkling of Germans who arrived in the second half of the nine-teenth century and have given the country colorful patches of Middle European "presence."

The Chileans belong to the upper third of Latin America

Progressive farmers discuss problems in Colchagua Province, Chile

in terms of output per person and per capita income but are the least willing to settle for conditions as they are. Present-day Chile tries, under a governing ideology of Christian Democracy, to carry through a "revolution in freedom" which is being watched with intense interest by all of Latin America.

The entire middle group adheres loyally to the Organization of American States but there exists a wide range of opinion among its members as to what this adherence means or should mean.

One of the more indicative touchstones of the attitudes of the nations in the middle was their response to O.A.S. action in the Dominican Republic in 1965. Attitudes on this occasion ranged from that of Paraguay, which early sent troops to the Inter-American Peace Force, to that of Uruguay, which undertook to criticize that force from the global forum of the United Nations. Peru, too, was critical, but kept its disapproval within the family. Venezuela was unhappy over what it considered too much interference in an American nation's domestic affairs. Ecuador was silent, preoccupied with a domestic crisis, as was Bolivia. Colombia was passive but polite, its interest focused on the possibility of a second transoceanic canal being dug through its territory rather than Panama's. Chile emerged as the articulate defender, on the embroiled island as well

A Chilean boy proudly displays his "project" raised under supervision of the Agriculture Extension Service

as in the councils of the O.A.S., of the human rights threatened by the conflict.

However widely the nations in the middle differ in character and policy, they have two basic concerns in common: they worry about being swamped by the power of the U.S., and they fret over becoming engulfed in the expanding economies of the big countries on their own continent.

As one Chilean diplomat put it: "We know there is legal equality in the inter-American system; we know the *Alianza* is a co-operative, multinational undertaking; we know the United States is a democratic country; and we know that neither Argentina, nor Brazil, nor Mexico means to establish economic dominance in Latin America. But the fact remains that unless Latin America is economically integrated there are dangers of the continent emerging with new extremes of rich and poor; and unless the Latin American continent strengthens itself through integration and political unity it will not offer a proper balance to the United States, and the inter-American system will remain, as it is today, lopsided."

A Colombian diplomat added: "We Latins are often charged with being too formal in our approach to the Organization of American States, too legalistic in our relationships to the inter-American system. This is true but the reason for it is that we try in this manner to hamstring the hemispheric giants with the ropes of law, to restrict their power with the obligations of form."

Venezuela has yet another approach to the problem of how to feel secure in a ring of big, even if friendly, neighbors. She believes the answer lies in an agreed political morality, practiced according to clearly defined rules. She wants the Organization of American States to work out a set of criteria which all members will use in recognizing regimes in the hemisphere and maintaining diplomatic and economic relations.

Venezuela knows that adherence to such a standard of political ethics would require the sacrifice of a measure of sovereignty from all the American nations. Venezuelan statesmen are willing to point and lead the way in making that sacrifice.

The eight nations in the middle are more ready than the big partners to trade some sovereignty for the rewards of economic integration and the securities of political unity. At least, so they say.

To date, their actions have not always matched their assurances. In the field of economic integration, it is the big nations of Latin America which have been most active and responsible in building up the Latin American Free Trade Association, and it is the small countries of Central America that have actually formed a common market of their own. From the middle group come the clarion calls for parliamentary conferences and political powwows which middle-group spokesmen tend to use as platforms for stirring rhetoric against one or another of the big partners, most often the United States.

Some of the nations of the middle group have also been the most demonstratively disloyal to the inter-American system (excepting of course Castro Cuba) or, as they would see it, the most anxious to insist on their rights. This despite the fact that the go-it-alone stance has never yet produced any desirable results for the defiant nation.

Bolivia, for example, walked out of the O.A.S. in a huff

in the early sixties over a territorial hassle with Chile concerning the headwaters of a river. The walkout changed nothing and Bolivia quietly slipped back into her seat a year later.

Uruguay, deciding suddenly to take off on a high-flying policy of her own in the Dominican crisis, found herself not only isolated from the rest of the Americas by her belligerent pose at the United Nations but escorted during her maneuvers at Turtle Bay by countries which obviously cared not one whit about the Americas and were using the Dominican crisis to promote policies of their own. Uruguay never said anything about her solo flight, but it must have been a disillusioning experience. Three months later a top Uruguayan delegation was in Washington to work out without fanfare the country's very real economic problems.

The most instructive foray away from the inter-American system, however, was the one undertaken by Chile's President Eduardo Frei, who in the summer of 1965 took himself on a string of state visits to Western Europe, including Italy, France, Germany, and the United Kingdom.

It was the first such official visit by a Latin American chief of state since World War II, and President Frei was received with full and formal honors wherever he went. There was much exchanging of extravagant compliments, elaborate diplomatic pleasantries, and assurances of mutual esteem. Only, when the chips were down and counted, they did not add up to very much.

President Frei had gone to Europe to see what he could do about rallying support for Chile's determined effort to build up her economy. What he was after was some technical aid, but the main need was for long-term credits and sizable loans at moderate terms. In response, Italy gently pointed out to President Frei the very narrow limits of what it could do. France reverberated with grand phrases and promissory assurances during the Frei visit, but a week later the De Gaulle government announced that it would cut down on its aid and credits to all developing nations not belonging to the French Union. West Germany, delighted to see a fellow Christian Democrat in office in the Americas, made plain its political approval and backed up that approval with the pledge of some technical assistance and a certain amount of credits, limited, however, to the purchase of German machinery.

The most rewarding stop for President Frei turned out to be London, where the cordial and sumptuous welcome he received was accompanied by a public declaration from the Wilson government that the United Kingdom fully understood, and completely backed, the action of the United States and the O.A.S. in the Dominican Republic.

Some days later the Chilean President criticized the Alliance for Progress in a public address in West Germany. A journalist asked whether the Chilean President had come to Europe to garner political backing for a Third Force in the Americas. President Frei denied this.

"We are part of the American system," he explained, "as a matter of historic and geographic fact. When we criticize this system it is not to weaken it but to perfect it. We are convinced that it is now functioning with great deficiencies."

President Frei is, however, as straightforward in his appraisals of his own country and continent as he is in his evaluation of the inter-American system.

In Latin America, where the political manner calls for the most elegant rhetoric or the most polite generalization, the spectacle of a major political figure calling a spade a spade is startling: shocking to some, a refreshing and encouraging change for others.

It took the courage of a President Frei to say bluntly to the culture-sensitive nations of Ibero-America that "education in Latin America is highly deficient," citing the figures and facts to prove his point. And no one before him in Latin American public life had dared to point out openly "the contrast between universities, sometimes with monumental buildings, and illiteracy and wretchedly inadequate schools . . . between circles of high standards of living, culture and sophistication and a huge mass existing in subhuman conditions . . . between the ultramodern city and the rural area of feudal and anachronistic structure."

This, President Frei insists, must not and cannot continue. "The people," he says, "wish to break with the old paternalism and ancient privileges but do not wish to be led into dictatorship of any kind. They wish to progress and create new forms of social life. . . .

"I dream of a synthesis of justice and freedom in an economy that is based entirely on man's ability, not on inherited factors of money, class, or race. . . .

"In Latin America, it is man who must be made great."

What role can the Organization of American States play in this grand new design advocated by President Frei?

Chile's ambassador to the O.A.S., Alejandro Magnet, sees the Organization as the natural spearhead of a democratic attack on the revolutionary tasks that lie ahead.

"The Organization of American States," he says, "can

*An unskilled worker
learns as he builds
in village near
Lima, Peru*

guide national collaboration, inspire intercontinental development, and promote economic integration."

From Ambassador Magnet's point of view, "Without integration Latin America has no future, and without Latin America the inter-American system has no future." Only a strong, prosperous, united Latin America, he is convinced, can be a true partner for the United States and only such real equality can achieve in fact the principles the O.A.S. Charter proclaims.

In achieving this equality, unification—economic unification now, political unification to come—is Ambassador Magnet's chief concern and should, he holds, be the chief preoccupation of the O.A.S. today.

So intense is his concern, reflecting the feelings of the entire middle group, that he seems unaware that no one disagrees.

The United States is in favor of Latin American unification, both economic and political. Vice-President Hubert Humphrey so said to the ambassadors to the Organization of American States assembled in the Hall of the Americas on Pan American Day, 1965. Mr. Humphrey even explained why the United States takes this position as a matter of self-interest. Our experience with Western Europe, Mr. Humphrey pointed out, proves that we do better business with developed countries. We profit from the unity, prosperity, and stability of our partners.

The big nations of Latin America are in favor of unification as well. It is they who most energetically search for the mechanisms to put the idea into practice.

The Secretary-General of the O.A.S. also emphatically endorses unification. In recent recommendations to the Council of the Organization, Dr. Mora suggested specific measures to foster both economic and political unity in the Latin American continent.

Still, the distrust of the large nations persists. It is so strong that spokesmen for the nations in the middle—and Chile has emerged as the most articulate of these—keep preaching to the converted.

"Big, modern scale industries make no sense unless they are geared to a large market," Ambassador Magnet insists. "There is no point in our competing against each other at this stage. We in Latin America must co-ordinate our industrialization, collaborate in our development.

"And," he reiterates, "we must unite politically. There

Ambassador Alejandro Magnet of Chile, Representative on the Council of the O.A.S.

cannot be any real association between the most powerful nation on the planet—the United States—and nineteen or twenty poor, underdeveloped, disunited countries."

One feels, listening to the earnest, intense Chilean ambassador, that the America he sees is as much splintered by fear and doubt as it is fragmented in fact.

Ambassador Magnet sees opposition where none exists, lurking enemies which on inspection turn out to be phantoms. With these spooks he creates a shadow-boxing drama.

He sets the scene:

"A tight, true Latin American unity would not be directed against the U.S. As matters stand today, the United States could support us technically and financially and we could back it politically and morally."

He spells out the conflict:

In Ambassador Magnet's vision, the interests of the two Americas are at present not identical but complementary and the relationship between the two continents had best be a kind of barter of progress versus security: economic support from the U.S. for Latin America, political support from Latin America for the U.S.

Finally Ambassador Magnet states the theme of his play —a big, global theme:

"The United States," he says, "cannot afford to lose the cold war in Latin America. We are her natural allies, politically, militarily, economically. The United States can lose

Andean village leaders travel far to La Paz, Bolivia, for news of Alliance plans for their communities

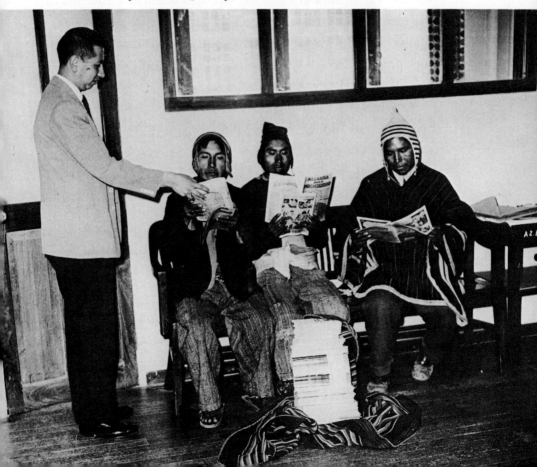

the world without losing Latin America, but it cannot lose Latin America without losing the world."

How great a part present fear and past-engendered pain play in this vision is illustrated by Ambassador Magnet himself, who concedes that he has difficulty erasing from his personal memory the time, just a short decade ago, when U.S. Secretary of the Treasury George Humphrey came to Latin America to declare, "I have not one penny to offer you." The same Secretary Humphrey, the ambassador adds, then gave $600,000,000 to Dr. Syngman Rhee of Korea, and stopped off in Caracas, Venezuela, to decorate dictator Marcos Pérez Jiménez for his contributions, as the citation read, "to the cause of liberty and free enterprise."

The drastic change that has taken place in U.S. policy since then has not escaped the ambassador. His desire that the change be quicker and greater still is understandable in the face of the facts and needs of his country and his continent. But he himself admits that bitterness and ingratitude tend to distort the view of what has happened already and of what is being done.

And so his play remains a tragedy, a tragedy which saddens him but, given his view of human nature, he sees no way of changing the script.

"In Latin America," he says, "we always look back. And humanity generally is inclined to forget the good and remember the bad.

"There is a saying in Spanish, that benefits are always written in sand, but injuries are carved in marble."

ANOTHER
MAJOR PROBLEM

Another major problem stalks the inter-American system, particularly the relationship between the United States and Latin America. And while it, too, has its roots in the past, it is very much a problem of the present —and the future.

The problem is trade.

As a general rule the nations of Latin America sell the produce of their lands and mines and buy manufactured goods. What makes this exchange wrong and dangerous for Latin America is that the prices for agricultural products and many mining products are going down throughout the world, while the cost of manufactures keeps rising. As a result, the nations of Latin America get less money for the goods they export and have to pay more for the imports they need or want.

International trade figures show that because of this imbalance in the world price structure the countries of Latin America lost $1,500,000,000 in 1958; $1,700,000,000 in 1959; and $1,500,000,000 in 1960. At a total of close to $5,000,000,000, this is more than the United States contributed to the Alliance for Progress during its first four years.

Measured with another telling yardstick, the loss suffered by Latin America because of price drops in its major exports added up to a total of $7,300,000,000 in the five-year period of 1955–60, which was just about the amount of money that flowed into Latin America during the same period from all sources—private foreign investment and aid of every kind. This includes loans which carry interest and have to be repaid, while the price loss suffered was, and is, irretrievable.

To the nations of Latin America it sometimes seems that they are in the same position as Alice and the Red Queen in *Through the Looking-glass:* they have to run just to stay at the same spot.

In the decade between 1950 and 1960 the peoples of South America made a major effort to expand foreign trade. They worked hard and succeeded in increasing their output to such an extent that they were able to sell abroad 41% more in volume than they had sold in the previous decade. But they did not get 41% more income. The price imbalance cut the return on their efforts by more than one third.

In the half decade between 1957 and 1961 the situation was even worse. Exports rose by 13% and the drop in prices during the five years exactly matched that percentage. In terms of net income—the money the nations of Latin America need to build roads and schools, to buy machines and equipment, or planes, ships and locomo-

At work on a coffee plantation in Brazil

tives, telephone wires and electric power plants—Latin America remained, after five years of hard and successful effort, with exactly nothing.

A Brazilian economist put it this way:

"In 1958, it took 2840 bags of our Santos 4 coffee to buy one locomotive. In July 1964, that same locomotive cost us 3052 bags of coffee. That's a difference of about 2600 pounds. The average tree produces a pound of coffee a year. And a lot of human labor goes into that."

While this imbalance constitutes a high hurdle to the economic development of the entire South American continent, creates major problems for the big countries and important ones for the medium-sized nations, it is literally a matter of life and death for the small members of the O.A.S. Every one of them depends on one or at most two crops for its livelihood. For Cuba, Haiti, and the Dominican Republic, the life-line crop is sugar. For Honduras, it is bananas. For El Salvador and Guatemala, coffee. For Costa Rica, a combination of coffee and bananas; for Nicaragua, cotton and meat. For all these nations the strength-through-unity economic advantage of an international organization such as the O.A.S. is as compelling a magnet as the military security it affords and the ideological appeal it holds.

An instance of O.A.S. importance to a small American nation is the sugar-producing Dominican Republic. Observers in the Republic say that one of the main reasons democratic President Juan Bosch had such trouble governing his nation effectively and efficiently was the fact that during his regime sugar prices were weak. The same observers claim that the turmoil which ousted President Reid Cabral and kept the island in chaos for months was set off primarily by sugar prices taking a dive. As sugar goes, so goes the Dominican Republic.

This seems too limited a view. The course a country takes is shaped by more factors than its economy; political and social tensions, plus the accumulated resentments and corruptions that had developed under the iron vise of the Trujillo dictatorship, certainly played their part in the Dominican crisis.

The vital importance, however, of the price of commodities for a small member of the O.A.S. can be seen in almost model form in Costa Rica, a compact, homogeneous nation of less than 1,500,000 people, with democratic traditions that are honored and democratic institutions that work.

"Let me spell the problem out," says Costa Rica's ambassador to the O.A.S., Dr. Gonzalo J. Facio.

"Any foray into the economics of Latin America must begin with one basic fact of life: most of our countries are raw-material and single-crop commodity producers. We depend for our foreign exchange on the export of meat, tin, copper, coffee, sugar, bananas, cotton, wool, petroleum, timber, cacao, sisal, tobacco, and the like.

"In Costa Rica our main export is coffee. Based on 1957 coffee prices, the five Central American nations suffered losses of $593,160,000 between 1957 and 1962, due to the steady drop in world coffee prices. In 1962 alone, the five Central American republics had losses totaling $187,700,-000. This loss in 1962 was more than twice the total U.S. economic aid to the five countries for the first fiscal year of the Alliance for Progress.

"Costa Rica herself lost an estimated $44,500,000 in 1962, while the total amount of aid in loans we received that year was $10,300,000."

Scanning the landscape with this kind of telescope produces a discouraging view. For some time discouragement did indeed afflict the peoples of Latin America and sap both their energies and their hopes. Then they got angry, and acted.

What made them angry was that, once again, they found themselves abandoned by the big neighbor of the north who had asked, and received, their co-operation when the shoe was on the other foot.

During World War II raw materials for the factories of the U.S. and food staples for its kitchens were scarce. There were shortages of all imported items, from tin to bananas, copper to coffee, petroleum to sugar, rock crystal for bomb sights to citronella oil for ointment. Latin America had these goods and could easily have manipulated the supply, hoarded it, or simply waited to sell and so driven up prices. It did nothing of the kind. On the contrary, it did its utmost to produce everything the United States wanted and needed, and it sold to the hard-pressed U.S. at fair and reasonable prices. In many instances it even accepted price controls suggested by the United States.

With the commodity of most immediate concern to Ambassador Facio—coffee—the Latin American nations went even further in their co-operation. In 1940 the coffee-producing countries of South America proposed that an agreement be worked out between producers and consumers in the Americas to keep coffee prices stable. The United States was quick to agree at the time, and in November 1940 an Inter-American Coffee Quota Agreement was signed.

When the war was over and the United States dropped its own price controls, it jettisoned at the same time all price agreements it had made with other nations in the hemisphere. This was done without consultation, negotiation, or even advance notice. The coffee agreement went overboard in that wholesale dismissal. As far as the United States was concerned, in 1945 coffee was on its own again and the coffee-producing countries would have to manage as best they could.

Coffee plantation worker receives his dinner of tortillas and beans

The result of this attitude was that the Latin American nations which had done their best to produce as much coffee as possible during World War II, primarily for United States consumption, suddenly found themselves facing overproduction and plummeting prices. If they were angry with the United States, the reaction is hardly surprising.

Coffee is an important as well as an interesting product. More countries are concerned with the buying and selling of coffee than with any other commodity. And the value of coffee traded among the nations of the earth is second only to that of oil.

For Latin America, coffee is more important still. It is

the continent's largest export. There is a saying in South America that "if ancient Egypt was the gift of the Nile, modern Latin America is the gift of coffee."

For the United States, too, coffee is not negligible. In dollar value it heads the list of U.S. agricultural imports. And the money that coffee-selling nations spend in the United States provides more than 460,000 jobs and almost $2,500,000,000 in factory and farm incomes.

We are indebted to the Arabs for coffee. There is a legend about a goatherd of Arabia who noticed that his flock of sheep was particularly frisky and frolicsome whenever he took it to graze off a certain small green bush with red berries.

Being of an experimental temper himself—this happened during the Golden Age when science, medicine, mathematics, and every form of constructive curiosity flourished in the Arab world—the goatherd decided to try some of the berries and see what happened.

What happened was that he found himself stimulated too, and spread the news.

The United States, it seems, is indebted to a lady for its cup of coffee. The first coffee import license on record in the U.S. was issued to a certain Dorothy Jones of the Massachusetts Colony in the year 1670.

By 1683 coffee had sufficiently taken hold of the public taste to produce a brisk trade in the fragrant commodity on the New York market.

Less than forty years later coffee was planted in the Western Hemisphere. The first harvest came in 1726. It was another century and a half, however, before coffee became of major commercial importance to the American continents. The beginning of the twentieth century found the Americas both producing and consuming the lion's share of the world's coffee.

By 1965 the United States understood that it was neither fair nor wise to abandon the coffee-producing countries of the Americas to their fate. On May 24, 1965, President Lyndon B. Johnson signed into law the full participation of the United States in the International Coffee Organization.

It had taken considerable time and extensive debate for the U.S. to commit itself to keeping the coffee peace.

The process began in the 1950s, when the coffee-producing countries of Latin America, finding themselves faced once again with falling prices, decided to band together in an effort to control their exports and thus stabilize the world market. They invited the United States, by far the largest consumer in the world, to join them, but were turned down.

They then approached other coffee-producing countries, mostly in Africa, to form a global protection league, and the African countries agreed.

At this point the United States woke up to the problem. Thomas C. Mann, an expert on Latin American policies who was then Assistant Secretary of State for Economic Affairs, persuaded President Eisenhower to agree to the formation of a Coffee Study Group composed of both coffee-producing and coffee-consuming nations. President Eisenhower concurred and the Study Group was established in the summer of 1958.

The group soon discovered that there could be no effective solution to the problem unless growers and drinkers of coffee got together on a global basis. Until this was done, coffee prices would fluctuate periodically and often wildly, to create forbidding price tags for the coffee-buying housewife in some years and economic crises for the coffee-growing nations in others. It made no sense to let this go on.

In 1962, now with the United States in the lead, the Study Group proposed an International Coffee Agreement.

That summer the coffee countries—producers and consumers—met at the United Nations in New York. The meeting produced its flare-ups and negotiations, accusations and defenses, disputes and settlements. In the end, via the tried process of give-and-take, an International Coffee Agreement to stabilize prices was drawn. It covers more than 95% of all coffee bought and sold in the world.

In July of the following year a provisional International Coffee Council was established in London, to administer the agreement. By December 27, 1963, forty-six countries had ratified the agreement and the Council became a permanent organization. It looked as if both coffee growers and coffee drinkers had good reason to wish each other a happy new year.

However, the United States, though it had ratified the agreement (the Senate gave its consent in May 1963), required enabling legislation from the House of Representatives to carry out some of the terms of the accord.

While the coffee countries chafed the House deliberated. It had important points to consider. Would the agreement drive up coffee prices for the consumer in the United States? Would the United States be limited to certain import quotas, running the risk of not getting all the coffee it wanted? Would the agreement restrict the United States in any other way in its international trade?

After a year of searching out the answers to these questions Congress was satisfied that the United States' interests were not imperiled by the agreement. The year's probe had also revealed to the legislators that the agreement helped secure the livelihood of 20,000,000 persons—12,-000,000 of them in Latin America, to which the United States was pledged in an Alliance for Progress.

On April 19, 1965, the House Ways and Means Committee submitted its report on the International Coffee Agreement and in a matter of days the full legislature had voted aye. Before another month had passed the President signed the agreement into law.

Up a few blocks from the Executive Mansion, in the House of the Americas, representatives of the coffee-producing nations of the hemisphere expressed their pleasure.

But Costa Rica's Ambassador Facio, reacting with the urgent sensitivity of a small, economically imperiled nation which can find protection and security only in international organization and through international agreement, swept his eyes around the O.A.S. Council and said:

"This settles the problem of one commodity. There are others. Let us go on from here."

TOUGH
DIALOGUE...

The summer heat hung over Washington in the week of July 21, 1964. In the Hall of the Americas the air conditioners hummed. The Foreign Ministers, meeting as the organ of consultation in application of the Inter-American Treaty of Reciprocal Assistance (the Rio Treaty), faced the greatest challenge hurled at the New World in a hundred and fifty years: international Communism, determined to conquer America.

When Latin America fought for her independence in the first quarter of the nineteenth century she had to contend with the resistance and machinations of a combination of European and Asian powers describing themselves as the Holy Alliance. Now, in 1964, a new combination of European and Asian powers was threatening to undermine American sovereignty and American institutions.

To the men meeting in the House of the Americas, it was astonishing and horrifying to see how little the situation had actually changed in a century and a half. The labels were different. They read "Marxism" instead of "monarchy," "dictatorship of the proletariat" instead of "divine right of kings." But the demands made were astoundingly alike, as were the promises. Absolute obedience was asked and in exchange salvation vouchsafed. The fanaticism was the same, too, as were the rigid organization, the devious tactics, the ruthlessness. Above all, the two alliances seemed to share the conviction that the New World was only an appendage of the Old, with neither the right nor the ability to shape its own destiny.

For a long time the nations of twentieth-century America had been unwilling to believe that there really existed such an alliance in their midst, and that it was determined to destroy them. By that week of July 1964, however, there was no choice. The evidence was too clear.

On July 26 the self-confessed Marxist government of Cuba, which had earlier proclaimed its disloyalty to the inter-American system, was judged guilty of intervention and aggression in the hemisphere and officially read out of the Organization of American States.

Twice before, in January and in October of 1962, Castro's Cuba had been warned that its attitudes and policies were incompatible with the inter-American system. This time the governments in the O.A.S. were asked to sever diplomatic relations with Havana; suspend trade, direct or indirect, except for foodstuffs, medicines, and medical equipment shipped to the island for humanitarian reasons; and cut off all sea transportation, excepting again "such transportation as may be necessary for reasons of a humanitarian nature."

Within a matter of months all member governments except Mexico had heeded the injunction. Mexico, taking a quaintly legalistic position to avoid adherence to the O.A.S. resolution, maintained that Cuba's subversion in the hemisphere did not constitute "aggression" in the meaning of the Rio Treaty. It was an odd position for the country that had suffered more than any other American nation from the first Holy Alliance's grasp for power in the New World.

With all American nations except Mexico concurring, the O.A.S. also warned the Castro government that the hemisphere would not sit still for further Cuban aggression.

"If it [the Cuban govenment] should persist in carrying out acts that possess characteristics of aggression and intervention against one or more of the member states of the Organization," the O.A.S. resolution read, "the member states shall preserve their essential rights as sovereign states by the use of self-defense in either individual or collective form, which could go so far as resort to armed force."

Don't try to undermine our system, the Americas in effect told international Communism. We will fight you with force of arms if necessary, and we will fight you together.

At the same time the O.A.S. in its resolution hopefully provided that Cuba's suspension could be rescinded by a two-thirds vote "at such time as the Government of Cuba shall have ceased to constitute a danger to the peace and security of the hemisphere."

The twentieth-century equivalent of the Holy Alliance had been a long time shaping up and sharpening its tools for the onslaught on the Americas. Throughout the 1920s, '30s, and '40s the Communist parties of Latin America openly took their orders from Moscow. They followed every zigzag of Soviet policy, including co-operation with the Nazis at the time of the Moscow-Berlin pact, and the complete doubling back on that track when Hitler attacked the U.S.S.R.

In 1945, while America's leaders were meeting at Chapultepec Castle in Mexico City to shape a hemispheric policy of peace and co-operation, Luis Carlos Prestes, then leader of the Brazilian Communist Party, publicly proclaimed that in the event of a conflict between his country and the Soviet Union he and his followers would side with the U.S.S.R. Within weeks the Prestes sentiments had been repeated by every Communist leader in the hemisphere.

In their domestic policies Latin America's Communists were equally unscrupulous. They collaborated with the worst of Latin America's dictators, among them Argentina's Juan Domingo Perón and Venezuela's Marcos Pérez Jiménez. On the other hand, they did their utmost to undermine every political group attempting to introduce social, economic, or political reforms in a democratic or peaceful manner.

During the 1930s and '40s the Communists in Latin America concentrated on seizing control of labor movements and running these for any dictator prepared to play their game. One of these co-operative dictators was Cuba's General Fulgencio Batista, who permitted the Communists to manipulate Cuba's trade unions as they saw fit, as long as they did not interfere with his regime or his stratagems. It is worth recalling that it was a Communist who betrayed the Castro resistance forces, when Castro still had a broad popular base and the backing of a wide spectrum of democratic opinion both at home and abroad, to Batista's henchmen. It was a Communist informer who foiled the first attempt to put an end to Batista rule.

Many top policy makers in the Americas knew this. They knew also that Fidel Castro apparently thought of himself, and certainly proclaimed himself with great frequency, as the new Bolívar. They found it hard to believe that such a man, with such experiences in his background, would be prepared to sell out not only his country but his continent, and be willing to lead a conspiracy designed once again to make of the New World a puppet of the Old. Because of this reluctance to accept so anachronistic and incredible a fact, the American nations were unwilling for some time to act against Castro.

The first time Castro agents actively assaulted another American nation was in 1960, when a contingent of Castro-ites landed in Panama. The invaders were caught, but the O.A.S. then preferred to view the assault as a border violation, to be disposed of by negotiation and good will. The Castroite contingent was persuaded to give itself up to Panamanian authorities and Panama, after interning the Cubans for a short time, allowed them to return home.

In the course of that first year after Castro took power similar assaults were directed from Havana against three more nations. In 1960, Cuban revolutionaries landed in the Dominican Republic, Nicaragua, and Haiti. They were all caught and in each case the matter was settled as it had been in Panama.

At that time Castro's tactics of subversion outside his borders were still raw and amateurish and perhaps he himself was not yet irrevocably committed to the Sovietization of the continent. By 1961, however, it had become evident

*Foreign Affairs Ministers at Punta del Este, Uruguay, applaud
the signing of the Charter for the Alliance for Progress.*

that Cuban sabotage of the inter-American system would
not confine itself to hit-and-run political adventures. At
Punta del Este, when the Charter was being written for the
Alliance for Progress, the Cuban delegation was more interested, and active, in trying to undermine the *Alianza*
than in working with it. Cuba, it seemed, had been cau-
tioned by Moscow to remember what the Marshall Plan
had done for Western Europe. The Communist International did not want to be nosed out of Latin America, as it
had been out of Western Europe, by progress and prosperity.

The refractoriness of Cuba at Punta del Este was followed a year later by the discovery of Soviet atomic missiles

on the island of Cuba, making obvious to a shocked America just how far Castro was prepared to go. The wave of consternation following this discovery was climaxed by a defiant declaration from Premier Castro that he was, and always had been, a Marxist.

The lines had been drawn.

By the middle of 1963 the O.A.S. had come to the reluctant conclusion that Havana was indeed "the regional center for subversive action by the international Communist movement in America."

And this, the O.A.S. noted, in both sorrow and anger, "is true not only in terms of the propagation of Communist ideology but also for the training of agents of every type for the countries of the hemisphere."

Reports reaching the O.A.S. at the time said there were a minimum of twelve Communist training centers in Cuba at which "students" from other Latin American countries received training in Marxism-Leninism, propaganda techniques, the use of arms and explosives, sabotage, and guerrilla warfare.

By the end of 1963, Havana-directed subversion in the Americas was no longer a matter of reports, hearsay, or secondhand concern.

On December 3, 1963, the democratic reform government of Rómulo Betancourt in Venezuela officially complained to the Organization of American States that the Cuban government was sabotaging governmental and democratic processes in Venezuela.

Communism's aim at the time was to prevent elections in Venezuela. The Communists were afraid that democratic reform forces would win at the polls and they regarded these forces as their main rivals for power. Communists within Venezuela went so far as to issue public warnings that they would kill anyone foolish enough to go to the polls. Their snipers did take potshots, and terrorists tossed bombs at voters' queues on election day, but even so they could not prevent an overwhelming majority of Venezuelans from casting their ballots. Nor did they achieve their other, primary aim of preventing a victory of the democratic forces.

The Venezuelan adventure was a test case for new Communist tactics in Latin America, replacing the unsuccessful direct-assault attempts of 1960. This time Havana had spared neither risk nor expense. A month before the elec-

Fidel Castro meets with students at Havana University

tions the Venezuelan government discovered, on a deserted beach at Coro, a three-ton shipment of arms, valued at about $1,000,000. The shipment contained mortars, bazookas, machine guns, recoilless and automatic rifles, high explosives and substantial quantities of ammunition, all hailing from Cuba.

The Venezuelan government took its evidence to the Council of the O.A.S. and demanded a meeting of consultation under the Rio Treaty "to consider measures that must be taken to deal with the acts of intervention and aggression on the part of the Cuban government affecting the territorial integrity and the sovereignty of Venezuela, as well as the operation of its democratic institutions."

The O.A.S. Council met the day the complaint was received but, still reluctant to accept even such incontrovertible evidence, appointed a committee to investigate the Venezuelan charges on the spot.

The committee, composed of one representative each from Argentina, Colombia, Costa Rica, the U.S., and Uruguay, went to Venezuela. On February 24, 1964, it reported its findings to the O.A.S. Council.

The findings sustained the Venezuelan charge.

On July 21 the Foreign Ministers of the Americas met and faced up to the inescapable: the Castro government was guilty of intervention and aggression in the hemisphere.

The decision to ostracize Castro and to sever diplomatic and commercial relations with Havana followed.

Since then the Organization of American States has taken additional defense measures against Havana-directed subversion.

O.A.S. (O.E.A.) units on peace-keeping patrol at Honduras-Nicaragua border in 1957. O.A.S. committee brought about peaceful settlement of dispute within a week.

In Central America—the nations of the Latin American continent geographically closest to Cuba and therefore most vulnerable to infiltration and sabotage—the Ministers of Interior met in 1964 to devise a joint plan of defense against subversion, a combined system of security. At the same time the Defense Ministers of the region created the Central American Defense Board to map military strategy for the protection of the isthmus. Within the O.A.S., sentiment mounted to make such combined efforts at battling subversion on a continent-wide basis.

The Special Consultative Committee on Security, which had been established by the O.A.S. in 1962, when Castro first proclaimed his Marxist convictions, issued a report in 1964 noting that Cuba's main "export" to Latin America was now subversion and that Havana was investing $150,000,000 a year in this "export."

The Security Committee pointed out that Cuba's actions in Latin America were no longer a matter of political persuasion or amateur sabotage but a long-range campaign by professionals to capture the continent. The Committee proposed that the O.A.S. establish immediately a technical department within the Committee to study Castro techniques and tactics and design professional methods to cope with them.

The Security Committee's concern proved only too justified. Early in 1965, Latin American Communist leaders meeting in Havana openly named their next Latin American targets and bluntly roughed out their tactics.

The Havana target list of 1965 was still headed by Venezuela, but contained also Colombia, Guatemala, Honduras, Paraguay, and Haiti.

The tactics remained the undermining of all democratic reform movements. Cynically, the Communist leaders called for the encouragement, wherever possible, of repressive regimes, and for a policy of intensifying the autocratic aspects of existing military governments, by creating civil disorder. In 1965 the tactic that had been tried unsuccessfully in Venezuela was still considered worth pursuing. The Communist program called for the prevention of democratic elections by the promotion of fear and chaos through terrorism.

The terrorism was to be two-pronged: aimed sometimes at specific political targets—high-ranking police and army officers or other public personages—but more often aimed at creating havoc of a more general nature by the dreadful

device of random bomb throwing in heavily populated
places.

Cuba's official position throughout these crucial years
has been a complicated performance of backing and filling,
defiance and denial, specious argument and political
braggadocio.

When, in 1960, the early, inadequately planned invasion
attempts failed in Panama, Haiti, Nicaragua, and the Dominican Republic, Castro quickly washed his hands of the
invaders.

"Not my men," he said, and took them back.

From 1962 on, while publicly asserting its commitment
to revolutionary Marxism, Havana claimed at the same
time that Latin Americans in Cuba were getting only
"technical training."

In 1963, having openly attacked and threatened the
Venezuelan government for months, as well as having
pledged publicly that he would make certain there would
be no election, Castro branded as "a U.S. lie" the charge
of Cuban intervention in Venezuela. The $1,000,000 worth
of arms found by the Venezuelan government, and
checked by the O.A.S. investigating committee, he dismissed as "fabrications."

In 1964, Havana admitted to—in fact crowed about—
10,000 Latin Americans being trained in Cuba for subversive purposes. At the same time the chief of Cuba's
delegation to the United Nations attacked the O.A.S. suspension of his country from the inter-American system as
inconsistent with the Rio Treaty.

That treaty, the Cuban spokesman at the United

Nations argued amazingly, provides for suspension only in the case of an armed attack.

In 1965 the Latin American nations made one more attempt to engineer Cuba's return to the American family. They met in Mexico to discuss the possibility of declaring Latin America a nuclear-free zone. Cuba was invited to the conference, but its response was: "We are interested only if the U.S. closes down her bases in Puerto Rico, the Virgin Islands, the Canal Zone and Guantánamo."

Cuba had, of course, no right to tell the United States what to do with military bases on her own soil, and was using this gambit only as a cold war stratagem. But the existence of a U.S. naval base at Guantánamo, on the shores of Castro's Cuba, is a fantastic anomaly. It is comparable to Communist China maintaining a base at Catalina Island, or the Soviet Union having a permanent military foothold on the Isle of Wight.

It is, however, exactly that anomaly, and the truculent truce maintained over it, which provides evidence that the last word has not been spoken in this toughest dialogue yet of the inter-American system. O.A.S. structure and attitude make possible continued debate and provide ample leeway for give-and-take, now or at any time.

When the Organization of American States suspended Cuba it not only left the door open for the Castro government to change its ways, it made clear in addition that, whatever Castro does or does not do, the O.A.S. considers the Cuban nation an integral part of the Americas that cannot be split off. The Cuban flag is etched into the seal of the Organization of American States.

On that torrid day in July 1964 when the O.A.S. said

"thus far and no further" to Castro, the notice was accompanied by a declaration to the people of Cuba.

The declaration emphasizes that "the exclusion of the present Government of Cuba from participation in the inter-American system . . . by no means signified any intention to deny the Cuban people their rightful place in the community of American peoples. . . . The free peoples of the Americas are convinced that the inter-American system offers to the Cuban people unequalled

Assistant Secretary of State Thomas Mann (center) and Secretary of State Dean Rusk talk with reporter at meeting of Ministers of Foreign Affairs in Washington, July 1964

conditions for the realization of their ideals of peace, liberty and social and economic progress."

Significant, and too often overlooked, is the fact that Cuba never slammed the door shut from her end either. While the severing of diplomatic and trade relations ordered by the Organization of American States met with the inevitable sour grapes comment from Havana that the O.A.S. was, in any case, "the United States Ministry of Colonies," Cuban spokesmen have never been so totally negative in their statements about the inter-American system as was Soviet-dominated Europe about the Marshall Plan and the various forms of West European military, political, and economic unity that grew from it.

In fact, when speaking privately—away from the major international soapboxes from which their voices carry quickly to Moscow and Peiping—the professed attitude of Cuban spokesmen to the inter-American system is not very different from that of Chile.

In the lounges of the United Nations, if not on its rostrums, Cuban spokesmen advocate first the economic integration of Latin America so that a balance will be achieved between the strength and power of the United States and the nations on the southern continent of the hemisphere.

In an off-the-record conversation a high-ranking Cuban official conceded, a little ruefully:

"We cannot really live without the United States. But we want to live with her on an equal footing. We don't want to be dominated politically, economically, or in any other way."

That same top-ranking Cuban spoke yearningly of a

restoration of normal relations with the other nations of the Americas and, while he accompanied his analysis of the present state of the hemisphere with the mandatory condemnations of the wickedness of "Yankee imperialism," he summed up this way:

"We are, after all, a part of America, geographically, historically, culturally. And for this neither Russia nor China is a substitute."

... AND POLITE
CONVERSATION

Is the British Commonwealth a substitute? Or the French Community? Or the Kingdom of the Netherlands?

That is the decision British, French, and Dutch Guiana and some of the islands of the Caribbean must make.

And so must Canada: largest, richest, weightiest of possible newcomers to the Organization of American States.

The resplendent mahogany chair in the Old Council Room of the O.A.S., with the crest of Canada carved on the back, has stood empty for a long time. Like a throne unoccupied, it has become a symbol blending question and challenge, accusation and hope.

Until 1948, Canada was in no position to decide whether or not she wanted to become part of the inter-American system. The rules would not let her. Inter-American arrangements and associations were confined to republics, and Canada, a member of the British Commonwealth and subject of the Crown, was not a republic.

In 1948 the word "republic" was changed to the more comprehensive "state." The new hemispheric body became the Organization of American States, not the Organization of American Republics.

This made Canada eligible.

Eligibility and acceptance are, however, not the same, and the process from one to the other can be long, slow, and troubled. It took the Organization of American States sixteen years to formulate the rules under which new members would be allowed into the Organization. And before the rules were finally set, some unkind and unwarranted words had been spoken.

Once the O.A.S. had decided, however, to tackle the issue of admissions, it moved with smooth speed.

On October 9, 1964, Argentina requested the convocation of a Special Inter-American Conference to deal with "a matter of interest to the hemisphere."

On November 4 the O.A.S. Council called the requested meeting, setting December 16 as the date and the House of the Americas as the place.

On December 16 the Foreign Ministers and representatives of twenty American republics met under the chairmanship of the Argentine Minister of Foreign Affairs, Miguel Angel Zavala Ortiz. Two days later they had drawn up the Act of Washington, which lays down admission procedures for new members of the O.A.S.

The procedures are simple. Admission is granted by a two-thirds vote of present O.A.S. members, after the new nation has officially requested admission and declared its willingness to sign and ratify the O.A.S. Charter and adhere to the obligations of the Rio Treaty.

Not eligible, however, are "political entities, whose territory, in whole or in part are subject prior to December 18, 1964, to litigation or claim between an extra-continental country and one or more member states of the Organization, until the dispute has been settled by some peaceful procedure."

Concretely, this means the exclusion, at present, of British Honduras, to which Guatemala lays claim; British Guiana, from which Venezuela demands some territory; and the Falkland and South Sandwich islands which Argentina says are rightfully hers.

Strong sentiments surround these territorial claims. Guatemalan feeling over British Honduras, for example, runs so high that she attempted, unsuccessfully, to postpone and obstruct the whole issue of admitting new members in order to forestall the possibility of an application by British Honduras.

As the Act of Washington was being drawn, a lead article appearing in Guatemala's official daily warned that the new rules would permit the admission into the American family of such "culturally different strains" as the British, French, and Dutch islands of the Caribbean— islands, said the official Guatemalan article, "which are characterized not only by the misery of their backwardness but also by their torpidity."

One of the "backward and torpid" Caribbean islands, newly independent Trinidad-Tobago, was sitting in as an observer at the O.A.S. drawing of the Act of Washington.

Trinidad-Tobago has, after Venezuela, the highest per capita income of all American nations south of the U.S. and by far the highest investment ratio of any country in the hemisphere. In the years 1950–62 it tripled its exports; its population is largely literate, and it has managed to maintain both political stability and interracial amiability despite the fact that it is a complex four-way mixture of African, East Indian, European, and Chinese strains. As an independent nation, its record of achievement is unmatched in South America.

Odd objections had, however, been voiced before in Latin America when the admission of new members was under consideration. A rather startling demurral was put forward at one point by Uruguay, generally the most democratic, literate, and culturally advanced nation of Latin America.

What, Uruguayan spokesmen demanded, would happen to the "Latinity" of the Organization of American States if all these other cultural strains were allowed to infuse it?

It was a strange argument to make. First, because the former French colonies and an important section of the Canadian population obviously partake of "Latinity." Second, because the substantial Indian populations of South America equally obviously do not. And, third, because the senior partner of the hemispheric alliance, the United States, does not either.

The argument did, for a time, rouse echoes in romantically Latin souls as well as in culturally jingoistic minds. In the end it did not prevail, and the Argentine Foreign Minister, in his statement closing the conference which had produced the Act of Washington, declared:

"We are anxious to see the arrival in our Organization of the new American states. They will strengthen our decisions and enrich the human composition of America represented in this Organization, by the contributions of communities formed in other spiritual fountains of the Western World."

As 1965 began the O.A.S. door had at last been pushed open. The next question was whether Canada and the newly independent nations of the Caribbean would now walk through it.

The answer seemed to be yes, they would, eventually. But the caution that had characterized the old O.A.S. members for sixteen years apparently had transmitted itself to the potential new ones.

In Canada, four months before the Act of Washington was written, Secretary of State for External Affairs Paul Martin had spelled out Canada's relationships with Latin America and his nation's stake in the O.A.S.

He pointed out to the Canadian people that the population of Latin America, at over 200,000,000, was now the same as that of the U.S. and Canada combined, and would be double that of North America by the end of the century.

Mr. Martin noted that Canada's trade with Latin America, at $650,000,000 a year, was substantial and growing, as were political, cultural, scientific, and personal contacts. He emphasized, too, that in international gatherings Canada had frequently functioned as "an honorary member of the Latin American caucus."

He reminded Canadians that they had been members of such inter-American technical organizations as the Inter-American Radio Office since 1937; the Inter-American Statistical Institute since 1943; and the Pan American Institute of Geography and History since 1961. That they had been present at Punta del Este, as observers, when the Alliance for Progress was launched and were, through contributions to the capital of the Inter-American Development Bank, participating in the *Alianza* effort.

"Membership in the O.A.S.," the Canadian Secretary of State summed up, "would present obligations as well as advantages for Canada. . . . It would not be without difficulties. . . . Nevertheless, I consider it to be part of the ultimate destiny of Canada as a country of this hemisphere."

But other voices, important ones, were heard in Canada at the same time and they did not concur.

While Secretary Martin was explaining Canada's positive relationship with Latin America, John Holmes, president of Canada's most important private foreign-policy organization, the Canadian Institute of International Affairs, told a prestigious audience:

"South America is about as remote from us as any continent, and the idea of a special affinity among the Americas seems to me to be based either on a totally unrealistic significance attached to the Isthmus of Panama, on the accident that a single explorer is commemorated in the name of our two continents, or on the fact that we were all once colonized from Europe.

"The argument for our interesting ourselves in Latin America ought not, I think, to be based on these dubious historical-geographic grounds."

The Uruguayan "Latinity" plea, which had so puzzled some members of the O.A.S., had earlier found an echo among the French segment of the Canadian population. In 1964, French Canadians were strongly advocating their country's entry into the O.A.S.

Commenting on these French Canadian promptings, Mr. Holmes said: "This [Latinity argument] is a little too racialist for me. Having struggled as we have to transform the Commonwealth from being an Anglo-Saxon empire into the model of a multiracial association, I think we should be wary about these romantic notions of Latinity. What French Canadians and Latin Americans may have in common which looks like Latinity is a mutual resentment of the arrogance of Anglo-Saxons. With that feeling I have as much sympathy as an Anglo-Saxon is capable of, but it is wiser to recognize it for what it is than to dress it up in cultural heresies all too redolent of notions spawned before the war in a sick Europe.

"Normans and Saxons and Celts, we have got so mixed up in the past thousand years that I find this talk about Latin temperament about as nauseating as the myth of the Aryan or the white man's burden."

Not all the factors slowing Canada's entry into the O.A.S. are matters of opinion or sentiment. There are practical problems as well.

Economically, Canadian statesmen, as leaders of a responsible "have" nation, ask themselves: "What can we really do for Latin America? How far will our resources stretch?"

Politically, there is the complex issue of Cuba. Canada maintains both diplomatic and commercial relations with Havana and believes it is doing a service to the Americas by keeping an objective listening post on Castro's island. If Canada joined the O.A.S. she would consider herself bound by the Organization's injunction to sever diplomatic and trade relations with Cuba. Is this wise now? Canada's leaders wonder.

They see a series of minor but nevertheless real problems as well. When the Act of Washington was written, the government of Canada did not think it had a sufficient number of diplomats with solid knowledge of Latin America to send south, or enough competent area experts in Ottawa to back and guide a string of new embassies in South America.

In 1965 there existed also a vague but prevalent feeling in Canada that the long lack of contact between Canada and the nations of Latin America had left a vacuum which would take some time to fill. Canadians had the impression that they did not know very much about Latin America and that this state of ignorance was mutual.

One senior member of the Canadian Department of External Affairs, who had served for some time as ambassador in an important Latin American country and could therefore speak from personal experience, put it this way:

"Perhaps we ought to postpone joining the O.A.S. until Latin America thinks of us in terms a little more comprehensive and accurate than that country of igloos and eskimos and the dashing doings of the Mounted Police."

The newly independent members of the British Commonwealth in the Caribbean, led by Jamaica and Trinidad-Tobago, feel considerably less remote from Latin America than does Canada. They are closer geographically and this, given modern communications, as well as the similarities of climate, makes for a sense of closeness, a recognition of relationships existing here and now.

Both Jamaica and Trinidad-Tobago expressed interest in joining the Organization of American States immediately after they became independent in 1962. For two years they were politely kept cooling their heels. They were permitted to walk the gardens of the House of the Americas, even to come into the house for special occasions, but they were not considered members of the family and were not admitted to family councils.

Jamaica and Trinidad-Tobago played the waiting role assigned to them with good grace. When their turn came, however, to respond to the invitation issued at last, they took their time about accepting.

In Trinidad-Tobago the Act of Washington was studied first by a special committee of the ruling political party, the People's National Movement, which was to report its recommendations to the party's central committee. The party, in turn, was to consider the issue on the basis of these recommendations and pass on its view to the Cabinet. Should the Cabinet decide that this was the right moment for Trinidad-Tobago to join the O.A.S. it would not act on its own but take the matter to Parliament.

"After all," said Sir Ellis Clarke, C.M.G., Trinidad-Tobago's ambassador in Washington and observer at the O.A.S., "we would want this to be a decision of the people, not just the governing party."

One year after the Act of Washington the Parliament of Trinidad-Tobago had not yet delivered its consensus. Sir Ellis, however, felt that Trinidad-Tobago had something to offer to the Organization of American States, and thought that his country would want to make its contribution to the inter-American system.

"For us, this is not merely a matter of jumping on a bandwagon," he said. "We want to consider carefully how we can best help strengthen hemispheric solidarity, security, and prosperity."

He paused.

"We do, perhaps, hope to be pace setters in this matter for the other English-speaking countries of our area," he added.

"After all"—and his eyes twinkled—"we do want someone in the Organization to play cricket with."

Cricket aside, substantial considerations are involved in Trinidad-Tobago's opting for its native hemisphere as against its traditional Commonwealth ties.

The islands are important producers of sugar. Under the British Commonwealth preferential trade system, they can sell their sugar each year at a guaranteed price. In joining the O.A.S., Trinidad-Tobago would trade this important measure of economic security for the risks of the international market or the unilaterally determined U.S. import quotas, which plague all other sugar-producing countries of the Caribbean and Latin America.

The sale of sugar is merely one major example of the sacrifices that would be involved in Trinidad-Tobago's adherence to the O.A.S. The islands would also rupture, or at least weaken, an entire network of economic, social, and cultural relations built up over a century and a half with the United Kingdom and the British Commonwealth which, on the whole, had worked rather well.

"Still," Sir Ellis mused, "we *are* geographically a part of this hemisphere and it is unlikely that a tidal wave will wash us away. They don't come that powerful even in the Caribbean.

"Also," he concluded, "we believe that in the final analysis geography is more important than history.

"The Americas have proven that, in the problems they have faced and the solutions they have found.

"We are aware that there is a trend throughout the world today toward regional groupings. And our group is America."

ONE HEMISPHERE,
INDIVISIBLE

And that leaves the final question: what is "America"?

Is it simply a geographic fact, as Sir Ellis Clarke thinks? A set of romantic superstitions, as Canada's Mr. Holmes holds?

Or is it, at least potentially, what Bolívar believed it should be: "The greatest region in the world—greatest not so much by virtue of her area and her wealth, as by her freedom and her glory"?

And if America is indeed what Bolívar supposed her to be, what are her responsibilities—to herself, and to the other parts and peoples of the planet?

President John F. Kennedy assayed these questions on that historic afternoon of March 13, 1961, when, in the East Room of the White House, he presented to Latin American ambassadors, to the Organization of American States, and to members of the U.S. Congress his famous proposition to make the decade of the 1960s one of unprecedented progress for the Americas.

Farmer receives title to eight acres of farmland during
President Kennedy's visit to Venezuela in 1961

On that afternoon President Kennedy said:

"We meet together as firm and ancient friends, united by history and experience, and by our determination to advance the values of American civilization.

"For this New World of ours is not merely an accident of geography. Our continents are bound together by a common history—the endless exploration of new frontiers.

"Our nations are the product of a common struggle—the revolt from colonial rule. And our people share a common heritage—the quest for the dignity and the freedom of man.

"The revolutions which gave us birth ignited, in the words of Thomas Paine, 'a spark never to be extinguished.'

And across the vast, turbulent continents, these American ideals still stir man's struggle for national independence and individual freedom. But as we welcome the spread of the American revolution to other lands, we must also remember that our own struggle, the revolution which began in Philadelphia in 1776, and in Caracas in 1811, is not yet finished.

"Our hemisphere's mission is not yet completed. For our unfulfilled task is to demonstrate to the entire world that man's unsatisfied aspiration for economic progress and social justice can best be achieved by free men working within a framework of democratic institutions.

"If we can do this in our own hemisphere, and for our own people, we may yet realize the prophecy of the great Mexican patriot, Benito Juárez, that 'democracy is the destiny of future humanity.' "

No meaningful voice has been heard in the Americas north or south to gainsay President Kennedy's appraisal of the meaning of the hemisphere, and of her domestic and universal tasks. But the problem and the challenge exist: how can these tasks be accomplished best and most quickly?

How, for example, does one powerful nation, representing 86% of the economic power of the hemisphere and 87% of its military power, work fairly and smoothly with a partner who is fragmented into twenty-one countries in various stages of development and has a wide variety of attitudes and requirements? How can such unequal partners meet America's responsibilities together and on a democratic basis?

What must be done so that the United States will overcome, once and for all, the highhandedness, the disinterest, and the rigidity which have for so long and so often marred the relationship with her partners in the New World?

How can the nations of Latin America rid themselves of their devotion to obfuscating rhetoric and put aside at last their game of "let's pretend," which has so effectively prevented the changes and efforts that have to be made?

Can the two American continents perhaps help each other to remove these subtle but tenacious obstacles to the achievement of good neighborliness and real progress in the hemisphere?

Behind the headline clashes and claims—and not always easily discernible—this apparently is happening in the hemisphere now: the gears are beginning to mesh, and the resulting sparks and nerve-racking noises are merely signs that the machinery is at last in motion.

In the U.S., within the past ten years, there have been major changes of thought and attitude about the New World neighbors.

In the mid-1950s it was still United States policy to oppose, or at a minimum disapprove of, national economic planning by the Latin American countries. The United States viewed with a jaundiced eye a major, active government role in economic development and was cool to sizable public investments.

These attitudes have gone. Today Washington policy makers understand that the nations of Latin America have neither the time nor the physical and social breathing space which allowed the United States to find and make its way through untrammeled private enterprise. United States policy makers and an overwhelming section of United States business realize now that different times, different conditions, different tempers require different solutions. At present the United States fully supports the nations of Latin America in drawing up comprehensive economic development plans and backs unstintingly large-scale public investments, including undertakings and areas which would be left to private enterprise at home. At the same time imaginative U.S. business and banking circles are taking an increasingly active interest in countries of Latin America where the overwhelming percentage of major enterprises are publicly owned and the greatest portion of investment is publicly made.

Other important changes have quietly taken place within the even more recent past. As late as the end of the 1950s the consensus in the United States was still that commodity agreements to protect the agricultural or mineral products of Latin America would be bad, or at least unwise, policy.

Today the United States is a leading member of the International Coffee Agreement. Moreover, policy makers are beginning to consider that, just as U.S. farmers need and get price supports to prevent them from becoming a drag on the national economy, so the agricultural nations of Latin America ought to be helped effectively by some device which will make certain that the hemisphere's economy is not endangered by a shaky foundation.

These are important new approaches but perhaps the major change in U.S. policies in the hemisphere is a matter of attitude and emphasis.

Latin Americans complained, with considerable justification for many years, that the United States was concentrating its interest and resources on the problems of Europe to the virtual exclusion of Latin America—as the hemisphere neighbors saw it, to their exclusion and at their expense.

Since the end of World War II some Latin Americans have harbored a special bitterness against the United States for the delayed, piecemeal help it extended to its New World neighbors, while it committed itself immediately and completely to Western Europe.

The Marshall Plan, these Latin American critics charge, poured into Europe $4,000,000,000 a year in U.S. aid, while even the Alliance for Progress, most ambitious and hopeful of U.S. commitments in the hemisphere, budgets only for an annual top scale of $1,000,000,000.

Especially resented is that Western Europe was given 90% of this in the form of grants and only 10% in repayable loans. While Latin America, less rich by far than Western Europe, gets only 30% of its U.S. financial help in outright grants, and the remaining 70% in loans that sometimes carry terms and conditions difficult for the receiving nations to meet. Always these loans contribute to the debt burden of the Latin American countries and constitute, at least temporarily, a further drain on their precarious balance of payments, a further strain on their hard-pressed economies.

In response to these Latin American remonstrations, United States spokesmen point out that Western Europe, in the Marshall Plan years, already had a base of highly developed industrialization, with competent technicians at every level, to make use of massive doses of aid, while many Latin American countries do not yet have the economic structure or personnel to absorb constructively the kind of financing which went to Europe.

United States policy makers also note in this connection that U.S. aid to Europe went into the reconstruction of countries which were suffering from the devastation of war, an undertaking to which no one could object. In Latin America, however, the processes of economic development have met, and meet still, with all kinds of resistance: from an entrenched Establishment which does not want change of any kind; from a sluggish bureaucracy that can and frequently does smother development; from lack of experienced technicians; and, occasionally, from the absence of responsibility or good will on the part of politicians.

Whatever the difficulties, however, there is no longer any inclination on the part of the United States to avoid or postpone the problems of Latin America.

At the Special Inter-American Conference held in Rio de Janeiro in November 1965 for the purpose of strengthening and streamlining the O.A.S., the United States delegation announced that it was authorized to pledge a continued commitment to the Alliance for Progress and all its aims, not only for the decade originally envisioned, but for whatever time and effort was necessary to have the Americas fulfill their economic potential and keep their social promise.

Earlier, President Lyndon B. Johnson had expressed his own feelings on inter-American relations.

"I began my government service in Washington under President Franklin D. Roosevelt," he told Latin American leaders during what he described as "a family gathering" at the White House. "And from him I learned that nothing is more important to the country I now lead than its associations with our good neighbors to the south."

For United States policy makers there is no doubt that the crisis in which the nations of Latin America find themselves now is as urgent, as valid—and as capable of resolution—as the difficulties which faced the countries of Western Europe after World War II.

More so, perhaps. The crisis can be met by providing the electric atmosphere of opportunity to millions of hemisphere citizens for whom the American dream until now

*Public health nurse gives a lesson in hygienic baby care
to rural family in San Salvador.*

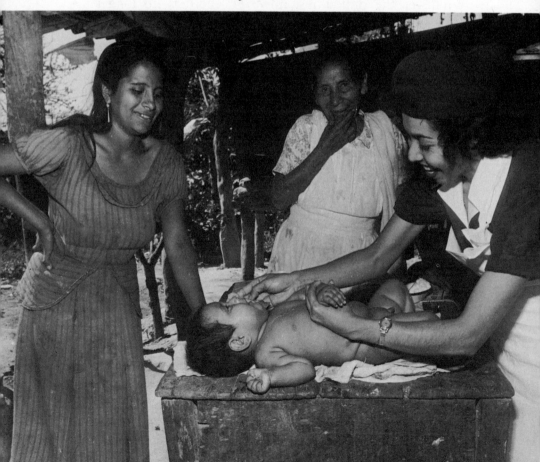

Rostrum of the auditorium during a Pan American conference

has been at worst a sham, at best an empty promise. And because these Americans are the most logical exponents of the revolution of expectation which is sweeping the world, the most natural participants in the wondrous spectacle of millions of people, whose lives have been dark and submerged, determinedly pushing their way into the sun.

In Latin America, too, fundamental changes in thought and attitude are taking hold.

Felipe Herrera, president of the Inter-American Development Bank, a Chilean who is occasionally described by Latin Americans as "one of the apostles of our progress," keeps after his fellow continentals to face up to the fact that "Latin America is not twenty nations; it is one great dismembered nation."

This means, Mr. Herrera never tires of telling Latin American statesmen and students, workers and bankers, farmers and industrialists, that their continent should be united, or rather reunited. And not *mañana,* but now.

"If we Latin Americans ignore the urgency of the situation," Mr. Herrera has warned, "we shall remain outside the margin of history. We shall see history pass us by, offering opportunities to other men, to other nations, to other regions that will not waste them through timidity, through cautiousness, through fear of the future, through conformism."

The unity or integration Mr. Herrera advocates so forcefully is not limited to the horizontal aspect of economic and political union. It involves also a vertical process, the integration of the neglected segments of society into the mainstream of Latin American life.

In both aspects of integration, the horizontal and the vertical, significant beginnings have been made. Vertically, the swelling drift of people from country to city, which in so many Latin American towns creates the unsightly blight of squatter slums, is at the same time evidence of a search for opportunity, the desire for a new and better way of life. More telling still is the fact that these newcomers to the cities are driven by the conviction that opportunities are available to them if they will go and seek them out.

This applies even more trenchantly to the Indian populations who, for the first time in the history of Latin America, are descending from their arid Andean heights to establish settlements on the outskirts of cities or on rich and idle lands.

These movements toward vertical integration, unplanned and often in violation of existing laws, present serious problems. But they are problems which the true unifiers and integrationists of Latin America welcome, or at least face, as proper demands and challenges of this time.

Horizontal economic integration, with all its complications, is also on its way. In Central America five nations have already formed an operative common market. In South America the Latin American Free Trade Association (LAFTA) is beginning to translate the theories of economic co-operation into initial practical steps.

Political union is taking a parallel course. In December 1964 the nations of Latin America gave themselves as a Christmas present the Declaration of Lima. Parliamentarians from all countries of the continent had come to discuss

New homes replace slums in Bogotá, Colombia.

unification on the political level. They resolved, in the Declaration of Lima, to form a Latin American Parliament which would work to promote political union. In July 1965 that Parliament met for the first time, with U.S. legislators attending as observers.

The presence of the United States at this first session of the Latin American Parliament was indicative of another important development in hemispheric history— the realization by the nations of the southern continent that the U.S. is, and will continue to be, a partner in their reach for a better life, a partner with a very special role to play.

Costa Rica's Ambassador Facio has defined that role.

"This great nation of yours," he told a U.S. audience, "pledged now to be our ally in progress, has to become the guiding force of liberation, liberation from poverty and ignorance, from backwardness and stagnation—in freedom.

"To help us achieve this," he added, "you—and not only the President and the government—have to summon your strength and your will, your feeling for the value of human dignity and freedom.

"You will have to renew your creative sense of history and make a real offer of your own to the millions of people of Latin America, not in the spirit of competitive bidding but as you would to your own fellow citizens.

"What we trust is that the United States will lead the American states into a real adventure of the spirit, into a great inter-American partnership with joint responsibilities and mutual obligations."

The response was quick to come.

Beneath the monument of Simón Bolívar is a living memorial to the man who dreamed of liberty and unity in this hemisphere—a meeting of Latin American Presidents in Panama.

Vice-President Hubert Humphrey pledged U.S. dedication to this "adventure of the spirit" and, with characteristic North American pragmatism, dubbed it "the politics of hope."

In this adventure of the spirit, pursued through the politics of hope, the Organization of American States must take an essential part. To play this part well, its powers will have to be strengthened and its structure made more flexible, so that it can respond more forcefully and quickly to the economic, political, and defense demands which will undoubtedly be made on it. But there is little doubt in the Americas that the O.A.S is the only suitable instrument which can convert Bolívar's vision of a New World without frontiers into the modern reality of a hemisphere indivisible, with liberty and justice for all.

*"Peace, like war, requires patience
and the courage to go on despite discouragement.
Yet we must go on.
For there is a world to lose,
a world of peace, of order, and of expanding promise
for all who live therein."*

LYNDON B. JOHNSON,
President, U.S.A.

INDEX

183

Grateful acknowledgment is made to the following
for permission to use the photographs in this book:

Aerolineas Argentinas, page 98
Brazilian Government Trade Bureau, pages 107 and 131
Wide World Photos, page 147
Pan American Union, all other pictures.

ABOUT THE AUTHOR

RUTH KAREN was born in Germany and educated at the University of London, the Hebrew University in Jerusalem, and then at the New School for Social Research in New York City. During the years she spent as a foreign correspondent, Miss Karen lived and worked in the countries of eastern and western Europe as well as in Japan and Korea. For nine years she was a correspondent for the United Nations; during this time she also wrote a column on the theater and one on economics, and innumerable articles for prominent magazines. Miss Karen has been able to gather firsthand the material needed to write this book on the Organization of American States, since she has spent the last few years in Guatemala, Central America, and has come to know the challenges and goals of this economic and political organization.

Writing is her full-time occupation when she is not engaged in her favorite pastime—meeting and talking with interesting people. She lives with her husband, an industrialist, in Guatemala City.